Abbondanza!

Abbondanza!

PLANNING AN ITALIAN WEDDING

LORI GRANIERI

CITADEL PRESS
Kensington Publishing Corp.
www.kensingtonbooks.com

CITADEL PRESS BOOKS are published by

Kensington Publishing Corp.
850 Third Avenue
New York, NY 10022

All Kensington titles, imprints, and distributed lines are available at special quantity discounts for bulk purchases for sales promotions, premiums, fund-raising, educational, or institutional use. Special book excerpts or customized printings can also be created to fit specific needs. For details, write or phone the office of the Kensington special sales manager: Kensington Publishing Corp., 850 Third Avenue, New York, NY 10022, attn: Special Sales Department, phone 1-800-221-2647.

Citadel Press and the Citadel Logo are trademarks of Kensington Publishing Corp.

Designed by Leonard Telesca

First printing: April 2002

10 9 8 7 6 5 4 3 2 1

Printed in the United States of America

Library of Congress Control Number: 2001099135

ISBN 0-8065-2294-1

*In memory of my grandpa Tony Marino . . . your cultural pride
and devotion to tradition live on*

Contents

Acknowledgments

I WANT TO EXPRESS my gratitude to the many individuals who helped me in the development of this book. Among them are Marie Conforti and her family; Chandi Wyant; the Bastianelli family; my friends and relatives—Mimi, Diane, Cindy, Tony—and everyone else who shared their stories, expertise, heritage, and prized family recipes with me. Thanks also to Jonathan Michaels for services rendered; to Bruce Bender for his enthusiasm for this project; and to the editors and staff at Kensington Publishing Corp. for seeing it through.

A very special thanks is due to my mother-in-law, Shelley, without whom our Italian wedding could not have taken place; to my parents, Toni and George, who made everything possible; to my adoring husband, Bobby, for his love, devotion, and support; and to all the "regulars" for being there every Sunday.

Introduction

SOME OF MY FONDEST CHILDHOOD memories were inspired by the customs of my ancestors. I didn't realize it at the time, but the big holiday parties with loud laughter, joyful music, and endless amounts of food, the routine Sunday gatherings around the dinner table and the time spent with family, were part of a culture I would later come to cherish.

In my adulthood, my Italian heritage became an important part of my identity. I enjoyed and appreciated the traditions, festivities, and, of course, the food. Over time I learned all I could about Italy, its culture and customs. And one evening I met a man named Bob (Bobby). It must have been fate because he was also of Italian descent. And we fell in love.

Once we were engaged, we agreed to have an Italian wedding, the kind I always dreamed about—loud, energetic, and fun. We secured a relative's backyard for the setting, our favorite Italian restaurant for catering, my parents' numerous Italian CDs for background music, and a fabulous florist and decorator friend to create a breathtaking "Tuscany Garden" motif, complete with grapes, vines, ivy, and garden roses everywhere.

During the planning, I spent a lot of time talking with Italian relatives, family friends, and acquaintances about Italian wedding customs. I learned about ancient practices that took place in different parts of Italy prior to the wedding, during the ceremony, and throughout the reception. I also found out about the customs at weddings of Italian-Americans throughout the United States and incorporated many of these traditions into our wedding, which made the wedding very personal and enjoyable for all who attended.

What makes an Italian wedding special? The high level of energy, the large size, the elaborateness, the enormous quantities of food, the lively music and traditional dances, the involvement of family and the overall upbeat festive nature of the affair: These are just a few of the special elements that make up an Italian wedding. But they aren't the only ones. Italian weddings can come in all shapes and sizes. How many of these factors you decide to incorporate into your own Italian wedding is entirely up to you.

Throughout this book, we will discuss various Italian wedding traditions, customs, and practices that have taken place over the years and how to apply them to your own wedding. You will gain an overview of the basic essence of an Italian wedding of characteristics common to all Italian weddings, and why they are important. You will read descriptions of the many details that make Italian weddings so special, and receive suggestions and ideas for creating your own Extravaganza Italiana. You will see just how meaningful, elegant, exciting, and fun an Italian wedding can be.

Also in this book, we will look at Italian wedding customs that occur from the very start of the romance—how a couple meets, becomes engaged, and plans their wedding, then on to what they will wear leading up to and on the wedding day, and then the actual events of the ceremony and the reception.

We will take an in-depth look at the important role food plays in an Italian wedding celebration: the elaborate several-course meal and the types of food commonly served for different courses—appetizers, entrées and side dishes, desserts, wedding cakes, coffee, wine, and other beverages. In addition to looking at Italian food as a whole, we will explore the cuisine indigenous to the various regions of Italy. Tips on hiring a caterer are also included. A later chapter features several Italian recipes, which you can prepare and serve at your wedding or use later for entertaining or cooking at home.

We will also look at music and dancing at Italian weddings, with ideas for what to play during the ceremony and all through the reception, as well as thoughts on hiring musicians, bands, and DJs. We will also cover traditional dances, such as the Tarantella.

Scenery is a big part of the Italian wedding, and in chapter 11, we will discuss how to set the stage to achieve that Italian ambience. Featured will be tips on Italian décor and how to best use a location to incorporate a captivating look. Provided are ideas for flowers, centerpieces, color schemes, and props. Also included are examples of various Italian wedding scenes, as well as descriptions of intricate details and how to duplicate them. Plus, we will look at creative ways to capture the distinct characteristics of several regions and cities of Italy. Unique touches for adding still more Italian flavor to your wedding, from creative suggestions for incorporating your Italian theme in seating arrangements and sentimental gifts to creating artwork and other Italian-inspired items for your celebration, are also provided.

And what if you want to take your Italian wedding on the road? Chapter 13 gives tips on how to plan a wedding in one of Italy's romantic cities, or closer to home in Las Vegas, New York, San Francisco, and Chicago. Information in this chapter can be used for planning your honeymoon as well.

Finally, we will look at life after the wedding, touching upon the honeymoon as well as on married life and celebrating holidays Italian style.

Planning and enjoying an Italian wedding is the experience of a lifetime. The memories of your wedding day will stay with you forever, setting up the foundation for the rest of your life as a married couple. And the time and care you take to plan your wedding will make all the difference.

Because I learned so much and had such fun planning my own wedding, I decided to share my experiences, ideas, and information with others, so that they may, too, experience all the joys of their own Italian wedding.

Whether you are a bride-to-be, a mother of a bride-to-be, or simply someone interested in Italian culture, I hope this book will help you plan an authentic and elegant Italian wedding. Abbondanza!

—L.G.

Abbondanza!

1

An Italian Wedding

THE SCENE IS SET: a spacious backyard with flower gardens and shady oak trees drenched in white light; tables set with white linens, fine china, elaborate floral arrangements scattered throughout the yard; a dance floor next to a stage arranged for a half dozen musicians. The gentle June afternoon breeze wafts through the air, carrying with it scents of fresh baked bread, roasted garlic, and a medley of aromatic herbs, spices, and tomato-based sauce.

Soon the guests arrive from the church and are greeted by the best man with cocktails. The band begins to play instrumental background music. The bride and groom are the last to arrive and immediately take center stage for their first dance— a waltz to a favorite old Italian song. Then they make their rounds of the tables, carrying a silver tray filled with little bags of Jordan almonds. Using a silver spoon, they hand each guest a treat from the tray.

Next, a fourteen-course meal begins with an antipasto, followed by course after course—seafood, pastas, meats—well into the evening. An enormous wedding cake is paraded to a table on the dance floor for the ceremonial cutting of the wedding cake, which is served with espresso, cappuccino, and an assortment of colorful pastries and cookies. Then, the festivities go into full swing.

Now the dance floor is packed, as bride and groom, bridal party, and family and friends dance the night away. The music is upbeat and the dancing vigorous. Various guests join the band to sing a song or two. Everyone participates in cultural dances like the Tarantella. After a sentimental father-and-daughter dance, the newlyweds change into departure attire and hurry off to their honeymoon, leaving the celebration to continue in their honor.

Think Big!

Most Italian weddings are wildly elaborate productions, painstakingly planned so that everything comes off virtually effortlessly, and where every guest—from the four-year-old nephew to the ninety-two-year-old great-grandmother—has the time of his or her life. There is always lots to see, hear, do, and eat. The key word is "lots"; the more of everything, the better. An Italian wedding is hardly (if ever) an understated affair. However, it can range in terms of how simple or extravagant you want to make it. Most of the time, the guest list at an Italian wedding is on the large side—anywhere from two hundred to six hundred guests is a common size. And all are treated as if they were guests at your home for Sunday dinner. This means that they are greeted with enthusiasm, served huge portions of food, offered a large selection of drinks, and provided substantial entertainment.

It's a Great Time They Won't Soon "Forgetta Bout"

If you have ever experienced a true Italian wedding, you are likely to remember it fondly. It was probably a highly festive and energetic occasion, with much activity, celebration, and participation. It likely invoked a full range of emotions from intense laughter to tears of joy. Every sense was engaged. You were delighted with beautiful sights (the flowers, lights, and décor), jovial sounds (catchy music, chatter, and chuckling) and the most delicious scents and tastes (assorted cheeses, spicy sauces, mouth-watering meats, and creamy sweets). Perhaps you indulged in the festivities so much that you went home exhausted. You remember it for the great time that it was, and have never forgotten the experience. Your wedding could be just like that. One for which your guests will have the time of their lives and talk about it for years to come.

The "Festa" of all "Festas"

An Italian wedding is a celebration true to the meaning of the word "celebration": to engage in festivities in honor of a very special occasion, or have fun. It's a good time for everyone.

A wedding is an occasion to rejoice the union of two people in love. What better reason is there to celebrate than that? And what better way to celebrate it than Italian style.

An Italian Wedding Is a Multifaceted Occasion

Italian weddings have something for everyone. While they are elegant and elaborate affairs, with traditional ceremonies and formal attire, they are also very comfortable and down-to-earth. People may be dressed in their best tuxedos and formal gowns, but that won't stop them from downing a few cocktails and dancing like a chicken on the dance floor. The church ceremony may be solemn, but the reception is decidedly festive with lots of noise and activity. Also, while old-school tradition plays a role, Italian weddings are still very hip and contemporary. Modern accommodations make guests comfortable throughout the extensive celebration, and newer songs, fashions, and decorative styles are sometimes added. And while the overall feel of the Italian wedding is that of a huge party, it is also very sentimental.

Made in Italy

Where else could the amazing Italian wedding come from but one of the most beautiful, romantic, and culturally rich countries in the world? Italy is the quintessential birthplace of all that is creative, ethnic, and authentic. It has brought us some of the best, from fine art to architecture to music to fashion to fine cuisine to celebrities. The Mona Lisa, the statue of David, the Coliseum, the Vatican, the Ferrari, as well as Vivaldi, Pavarotti, Dean Martin, Sophia Loren, Rudolph Valentino, Versace, Marlon Brando: all are Italian.

The physical characteristics of the country are intriguing with its agricultural features, stunning mountains, and breathtaking Mediterranean coastlines. Italy is modern and industrialized, yet antique and unchanged. Its people are like no other in the world, known for their animated, charming, and charismatic nature.

Everyone has a point of reference when it comes to Italy: spaghetti, pizza, Chianti, coquetry, soccer, bacci, opera, pasta, meatballs, olive oil, the Pope, fine leather products, passion, romance, family. Most people have at least one favorite Italian restaurant. Nearly all things Italian are world-renowned, and it is not difficult to familiarize people with the overall feel of Italian. Most understand the essence of Italy, even if they have never been there, don't have an Italian background, or haven't studied Italian culture.

Many already know that Italy is the boot-shaped country with two smaller islands near the toe, and that the land is made up of many cities within different regions that each have their own charm and unique characteristics. For example, when one thinks of Venice, gondolas, canals, and bridges come to mind. Rome conjures up images of the Pope and the Sistine Chapel. And Tuscany recalls to mind rolling hills, vineyards, and cottages.

Italian Culture

Italian culture is traditional and family-oriented, and incorporates many rituals based on the Catholic Church and ancient ancestry. And many aspects of Italian culture are seen all over the world. No matter where they go, Italians bring a part of Italy and its customs with them. As Italians have migrated away from the motherland, their lifestyles and strong bonds with tradition have been treasured and upheld with honor, and passed down from generation to generation, each taking pride in carrying on these traditions.

The Italian Zest for Life

Italians live life to the fullest. They have a passion for everything they do and they often demonstrate this passion through frequent celebrations with family and friends. Get-togethers almost always revolve around a meal, and include people of all ages, loud conversation, laughter, and fun.

Italians put their whole hearts into entertaining, which is reflected in the success of the event. Think about your favorite Italian restaurant. You probably enjoy going there as much for the hospitality as for the fine cuisine. So, whether it's the Sunday family dinner or the elaborate Italian wedding, the feast is always hearty; the mood always festive.

In Italy there are hundreds of festivals that take place every day in honor of saints, a particular village, a good harvest, historic events, or to highlight products, food, and local artists' work. In Venice in the spring, Carnival is celebrated with elaborate costumes and masks. There is always reason to have a good time.

The Importance of Family

In addition to their passion for life and living it fully, Italians are known for their commitment and loyalty to family. To Italians there is no deeper bond than family and they take that seriously. Elders are respected, children are included in celebrations, and everyone looks out for one another. Italian families spend a lot of time together. Family members turn to one another in times of need and can usually depend on each other.

As children grow up, they realize more and more how important their relatives are and they do whatever they can to keep familial connections alive. Of course,

Italian weddings, judging by the number of guests who attend, are a prime example of how strongly these family ties are maintained.

Italian Expressiveness

Italians are known for being very expressive. You don't have to guess what they're thinking because they'll tell you. Italians also don't try to hide their emotions. If they feel sad, they cry; if they're mad, they yell; if they're happy, they smile; and so on. They are often animated storytellers, and speak with excitement and full voice, hand gestures, and facial expressions as they describe every detail. Italians are very passionate people. They feel deeply, they enjoy immensely, and they emote regularly. Quite often, a handshake isn't enough. There's a lot of hugging and kissing that goes on between Italians. And they are very welcoming to new visitors. It's no wonder that Italian weddings are so fantastic!

An Italian Wedding Story

Marie Pulli was born and raised in a town called Cortele, just below Naples. After finishing fashion design school in Milan in 1963, the twenty-year-old traveled to the United States to visit relatives. Marie had intended to go back to Italy to begin a dressmaking career, marry her then-boyfriend, and live near her father's home. Instead, she met an Italian-American named John Conforti, fell in love, and got married in the States. They had a traditional Italian wedding—a Catholic ceremony and a festive reception with an open bar, full feast, an Italian band, and 300 guests.

Growing up in Southern Italy, Marie had attended numerous weddings, all of which featured traditional elements.

"Weddings in Italy involved the whole town," Marie explains. "You had a church wedding and people would stand outside and throw lire in the street and the kids would go and pick them up. There would always be a godfather who would give the bride a ring of aquamarine or her birthstone. This godfather, who was an intimate acquaintance or relative of either the bride or groom, also served as a witness or the best man. The altar was covered with flowers and the bride would give a bouquet of flowers to the statue of the Virgin Mary.

"After the couple left the church, people would throw rice, Jordan almonds, and money and follow them to the reception. There would be a receiving line and then an intimate dinner was served inside the home of the bride's parents, while the rest of the townspeople would be served appetizers and drinks outside. The meal included some sort of pasta, and courses like veal cutlet and eggplant Parmesan, served with bread rolls and salad. The wedding cake was usually a rum cake or a fruit cake and was served with coffee, liqueurs, and sweets people would make for the wedding, like aralli and biscotti.

"After dessert, there was music and dancing, including ballroom dances like the tango, waltz, polka, and Tarantella. We grew up with these dances and automatically knew how to do them. Everyone would join in, from the children to the old people.

"Italian weddings today are similar to those of the past, but nobody has a procession in the street with all the cars. The reception often takes place at a restaurant with an ocean view. In Southern Italy, every place has an ocean view."

Why Plan an Italian Wedding?

WHY IS HAVING AN Italian wedding important to you? Perhaps you want your Italian heritage in your wedding. Or perhaps you are simply looking for a unifying theme to make your wedding special. Maybe you don't want to have a full-out Italian wedding, but you'd like to use certain aspects, such as food, scenery, or one or more Italian customs in your celebration. No matter how much Italian tradition you decide to incorporate into your own wedding, the elements you do use are sure to give your special day an added dose of festivity.

A wedding by nature is a joyous occasion. It is the celebration of love and commitment between two people. It is the joining of family and friends. Most couples who decide to get married are excited about their decision, and want to share this excitement with their loved ones. For some that means having a very small gathering for family and close friends; for others it means inviting everyone the couple has ever known. Large or small wedding, planning to spend the rest of your life with someone is an event to celebrate.

In recent years, the biggest shift in weddings has been to personalize the wedding celebration. These days, more and more couples have been tailoring their weddings to their individual tastes, hobbies, personalities, and cultural backgrounds, and infusing these aspects of themselves into the celebration, from the ceremony to the reception and beyond. This makes the celebration unique and meaningful.

An Italian Wedding Is Meaningful

If you are of Italian descent, using Italian traditions and customs in your wedding will make it that much more significant to you and your guests. And if you are like most Italians, your family means a great deal to you, so you probably will be thrilled to take their preferences into consideration.

The daughter of Marie Conforti, the woman whose Italian wedding story wrapped up the last chapter, also had an Italian wedding. It was very important to Marie, who was born and raised in Southern Italy, that her daughter have an Italian wedding. Barbara was more than happy to oblige, and, of course, the wedding was beautiful.

Barbara and her bridesmaids met at her parents' home, where they dressed and had their hair and makeup professionally done. Barbara's mother, a seamstress educated in Milan, designed and made Barbara's wedding dress, made of white pure silk and thousands of beads, with a twenty-foot train. A limousine picked up the girls and took them to the church. Barbara had attended the parish's Catholic school from first through eighth grade. Barbara's father gave her away at the traditional hour-long ceremony and mass.

A reception for 350 guests followed at a hotel banquet room. There, guests enjoyed endless Asti Spumante, dined on London broil, pasta dishes, salad, and breads. For dessert, guests were served slices from a multilayered wedding rum cake, along with spumoni and five huge trays of colorful Italian cookies baked by friends of the bride's family.

For the wedding favors, Barbara's mom went to Italy and bought 175 small Capo Monte vases (which are miniature porcelain pitchers with roses painted on them) and put five to seven—because odd numbers are good luck—Jordan almonds inside and tied them up with ribbon and tulle. A two-piece Italian band played a combination of old Italian songs and modern music. The bride and groom danced their first dance, Barbara and her dad danced a father-daughter dance, and guests joined in for the Tarantella.

Having an Italian wedding means a lot to the parents, grandparents, and other close relatives of the bridal couple. It further links them with their Italian roots, brings back fond memories, and gives them a sense of pride. Plus, it lets them know that this heritage that they have passed down to the younger generations is as cherished as it always has been, and that this couple will pass it on to future generations. These traditions are part of them and connect them to where they came from.

The significance of an Italian wedding is far-reaching. Of course, it means a lot to the couple about to be married, their parents, and immediate family. But it is also a momentous event for other Italians in attendance who might be distant relatives of the couple, or friends with Italian roots. Your wedding is likely to evoke their own happy memories of Italian weddings, celebrations, and traditions. They will likely be touched by nostalgia and delighted to share in your celebration of culture.

An Italian wedding is a meaningful experience for everyone who attends—Italian or not. It gives everyone an opportunity to learn more about the couple and the couple's heritage and makes the day more special.

For many Italian couples getting married, incorporating their heritage into their wedding day is a way to stay connected with their cultural background. Italians treasure their heritage and incorporate it into everything. An Italian wedding is a true celebration of who you are, where you came from, and where you are going. Planning an Italian wedding will bring you in touch with your precious culture, giving you an in-depth look at your ancestry throughout the process.

An Italian Wedding Is Romantic

Because of their traditional and elaborate nature, Italian weddings are considered extremely romantic. They usually feature all of those things little girls dream of when fantasizing about their own weddings. Italy is known for being one of the most romantic countries in the world, and Italians carry with them the romance and eternal charm of Italy, with old-fashioned practices filled with sentiment.

A Central Theme Is Unifying

Many couples choose a theme around which to center their wedding. When a wedding is planned around a theme, the details, such as invitations, music, and menu work together to create a unified effect. It takes a lot of planning to coordinate a wedding around a theme, but the planning makes the wedding process easier. When you have a central theme in place, you eliminate many variables, such as types of food to serve or party favors to give. This gives you a more manageable framework from which to focus on the details that really matter. You will still have many choices to make, including which aspects of the theme to include and how to incorporate it.

Your Italian wedding can be orchestrated like a scene from an Italian movie, with all of the elements working so well together it will seem to your guests that the entire process was effortless; however, at the same time, they will notice the attention to detail and appreciate the overall effect. For you, the day will seem effortless because you will have all the details under control. Organizing around a central theme may seem time consuming in the planning stages, but it will help you stay organized and focused on your goal.

An Italian Wedding Is Emotional

An Italian wedding is a highly emotional affair. Someone once said, "Italians feel everything more than anyone else." That's a generalization, of course, but it bears some truth. Italy is known for its romance, and Italians are known to be passionate people. Their language seems more magical than any other, their wine more red, their art more inspired, their music more intoxicating, their food more rich, and their love more deep. Italians may or may not feel more than most, but they typically emote more. At an Italian wedding, you can bet there will be tears of joy, wild excitement, and lots of laughter, hugging, kissing, well-wishing, and passionate good-time having.

An Italian Wedding Is Fun

Italian celebrations are filled with gusto! Italian weddings are extraordinarily festive events with all the ingredients for a wonderful time. Just think: everyone you care about together for a huge feast, dancing to great music, and having a great time. This alone is reason to have an Italian wedding!

3

What Traditions Are Made Of?

ONE OF THE THINGS that make Italian weddings so memorable is the incorporation of customs that symbolize good luck and good times, such as the good-luck charms worn or carried by the bride and groom. Others are tied in with religion, such as the ceremony itself and holding the wedding in the Catholic church, and ancient beliefs, such as marrying in preferred months and avoiding others. While some traditions are antiquated and rarely, if ever, practiced anymore, others flourish. Some customs have developed over recent years and reflect modern advancements such as the use of stretch limousines. Many Italian wedding customs are shared by various cultures worldwide, while others are completely Italian and specific to Italian weddings.

Your reasons for including Italian wedding customs in your celebration will be based on many factors; what's most important is the significance they have for you. For example, you may include a special dance that has been in your family for many years, or you may partake in a pre-ceremony ritual that is commonly practiced by other Italians because you feel it has a personal significance. You may decide to serve the cuisine of the Italian region from which you descended. You may choose to include a certain Italian song because you like its festive tempo. Having many choices is part of the fun.

Italian Wedding Tradition Sources

Most Italian wedding traditions stem from these sources: religion, superstition and beliefs, and fun. Still others have been influenced by region and individual families. While many of the wedding traditions featured in this book are imported from ancient Italy, others have come from American modern times and from other cultural backgrounds. Some of these traditions may have originated in Greece or Germany, but over time have become part of the Italian wedding.

Religion

As with the practices of most cultures, many Italian traditions are rooted deeply in religion, specifically the Roman Catholic church. With the Catholic headquarters in Rome, a great majority of Italians are Catholic. Most Italian wedding ceremonies take place in a Catholic church and feature many religion-based rituals, which we will discuss further in chapter 7.

Superstitions and Beliefs

As is true with many cultures, Italian wedding customs are rooted in superstition and are concerned with bringing good luck and avoiding bad. And why not? If you have the opportunity to partake in a simple and harmless activity—no matter how silly it might seem—that may possibly sway fate to your favor, what's the harm? Such superstitions are worldwide, relating to when the wedding can take place, where each person in the ceremony must stand, what people can and cannot wear, and so forth. It is thought that not following these basic practices may bring bad luck to the marriage.

What are some of the most common wedding beliefs? How about "something old, something new, something borrowed, something blue (and a sixpence in her shoe)" for an English bride? Or that the bride should wear a white gown because it symbolizes purity, simplicity, and innocence. There's an old saying that suggests being married in white means the couple has chosen right, while being married in gray, black, red, green, yellow, or pink can mean trouble ahead. Oddly, however, it is okay to be married in blue as blue is considered to be a "lucky" wedding color.

Many believe that it is bad luck if the groom sees the bride's wedding gown before the wedding day, or if the groom sees the bride in her wedding gown before the ceremony, and if the groom drops the wedding band during the ceremony.

Luck and the Gods

Luck has always played a large role in Italian culture, starting with the ancient Romans who worshipped gods and goddesses to bring them luck. One of the "luckiest" goddesses was Fortuna, the symbol of fertility, often shown with a wheel that she spun, showing failure or success to mortals. Fortuna also had a rudder with which she steered people's lives. The word "fortune" derives from the name of this goddess.

Juno was the protector of women and the goddess of marriage and childbirth. She was the queen of the gods, and the wife of Jupiter. To this day, many people consider the month of June, which is named after Juno, to be the most favorable time to marry.

For the Fun of It

Some Italian wedding traditions are practiced for no other reason than for fun. These customs may have originated in the early days as a celebratory part of the wedding and are still carried out today. We'll get into many of these later in the book.

Customs Used in Italian Weddings

Some Italian wedding customs can be added to the wedding celebration simply, while others take more planning, thought, time, and resources. Many of the traditions in the ceremony will be incorporated automatically—the Catholic wedding ceremony is full of rituals that become part of the Italian wedding ceremony tradition.

Other traditions require participation from the bride, groom, best man, family member(s), or hired help. In some ceremonial customs, which we look at more closely in chapter 7, the bride and groom may wear and carry various items for good luck, while during the reception, the best man is expected to act as a host. And in most cases, traditions related to food and music are carried out by caterers and musicians.

The Importance of Traditions

People use tradition in their wedding celebrations for many reasons, but the most substantial reason is to hold on to and celebrate their culture. They may also participate in wedding rituals for superstitious reasons, and because these rituals are familiar and comfortable. There is something warm, inviting, and nostalgic about partaking in cultural customs. And a wedding is certainly a time for everyone to feel warm, comfortable, and welcome.

In the chapters that follow, many Italian wedding traditions will be explained, and suggestions, tips, and ideas on ways to include them in your wedding will be provided. Will including any or all of these wedding customs bring good luck to your marriage? Who knows. But one thing is certain: you will certainly have fun participating in these customs and traditions.

4

The Italian Engagement

A WEDDING DOES NOT consist only of the events of the day of the big party. There are certain events that must occur first that are all part of the celebration of marriage. A man and a woman meet, fall in love, and become engaged. After the engagement, there are many pre-wedding planning activities that the couple and their families take part in. In this chapter, we'll look at how an engagement occurs in traditional Italian style.

In the old days, arranged marriages were common throughout Italy, and while some may still take place today, they are not that common. And even when they do occur, the bride and groom have usually at least met or even gotten to know each other before someone suggests the possibility of marriage. Even better, it's generally the young couple themselves who come up with the idea. But even then, the parents still believe it's their duty to agree to the union or not.

In Italy, parents often play a significant role in matchmaking, and do all they can to secure the right mate for their child. After all, Italian parents want the best for their children and they are not shy about letting their preferences be known. Whether or not children will follow their parents' wishes is another story. In the old days, most children had to do as their parents said because they were financially dependent upon them. Not to mention that family has always played a significant role in Italian life, and to go against one's parents' wishes wasn't a common occurrence. Most children learned to respect and even fear their elders, and did whatever they could to please them. But at the same time, parents weren't unreasonable about who they chose for their children to marry because they wanted their children to be happy. Therefore, parents and children often agreed on the marital arrangement. Of course there were exceptions.

These days, people all over the world are getting married at an older age, and therefore, are not always dependent on their parents at the time they marry. Respect for parents still means they will take their parents' approval or disapproval seriously.

From ancient times to Italian life today, there have been many traditions passed on regarding how a couple meets and becomes engaged. There are also several ways you can incorporate Italian tradition into your own engagement.

A Couple Meets

Long ago in Italy, young people typically grew up in villages or towns where everybody knew everybody else. The person someone would eventually fall in love with was someone they'd probably known since kindergarten. Their parents knew each other, and probably grew up together as well. And there weren't many new prospects to choose from, unless a new family moved into their village. Soon enough, the new people would meld right in with everyone else.

Throughout school, the future couple may have had crushes on one another or just been good friends—or they may have even hated one another. Like many kids who have lived in the same town their whole lives, attended the same schools together, and, for the most part, grown up together, they know everything about each other—which can be a comfort or a bore. Either way, it was accepted.

As the kids grew into teenagers, they may have developed an attraction to each other. And while they may have made this known to their parents, it is more likely that they would keep it quiet. Often their parents would find out anyway: In a small town, word travels fast. Once parents found out about the attraction, they'd keep a close eye on the kids, making sure there was no chance of them being alone together—especially the parents of the girl. If the children were at or approaching marriage age, the parents would make contact with the other family to discuss the possible future. After such an encounter, assuming there was approval on both sides, the boy's parents would inform him of the mutual approval and start discussing with him plans for the marriage proposal.

In other cases, the parents might have already had another spouse chosen for their child, or another agreement may have already been made. In this case, there would be conflict between parents and children. If an agreement had already been made, the children often didn't have much say. However, in instances when there hadn't been any official agreement, and the parents preferred another spouse for their child, the parents might give in depending on the quality of the child's choice.

In cases when the parents didn't already know the family of their son's or daughter's beloved, they would make a point to check the background. Often the girl's family researched the boy and his family by checking police records, talking to people who knew the boy, or even by hiring a private investigator to follow him around. If the young man seemed to come from a good family and have a clean background, the parents approved. Otherwise, they did what they could to stop the wedding, including refusing to pay or attend.

Only those with financial security were likely to have lavish weddings. Weddings are expensive, and the parents had to be able to pay for an appropriate one with all of the trimmings. Plus, a couple had to have the means for their own home that was as nice as or better than their parents' home. This meant that the parents had to have enough money to give the couple a suitable home on top of the cost of the wedding.

There were some pretty strict guidelines for who could end up with whom. If a girl was poor, she could not marry someone rich; the same held true for the groom. People always married within their class and educational background. In some parts of Italy, this class system still exists.

Age also played a role. Long ago, people typically got married at about seventeen to nineteen; now, even in the most old-fashioned Italian towns, the average marrying age is twenty-six. If a woman was past thirty, no one would marry her, unless an older man's wife died and he opted to marry a more mature woman. In Italian, an older unmarried woman was called a "ditello," or spinster.

Although there are still small villages in Italy that continue the old ways, in most cases, men and women meet in millions of places and ways: in college, at work, in the park, at a bar, at church, at sporting events, on the street, through friends, and yes, sometimes through their parents and even friends of their parents.

Italian parents continue to play a role in the process of selecting the right mate for their children—or at least they try to. How many times have you met an Italian woman who has insisted that her son (or daughter) would be perfect for you? Or has your own mother ever said that to you?

As we understand the process, it is customary to see the person we are interested in again and again in social situations. We understand this as dating, or something couples do to get to know each other before moving into a serious relationship. But in old-time Italy, this process did not exist.

Dating in Italy

There was a time that dating was forbidden in Italy. It was inappropriate for a young man and woman to be alone together before they were married. Unless they snuck around to see each other, the first time a couple would be alone together was on their wedding night. Boys and girls who were interested in one another could see each other at school or in large groups. Sometimes they could be together only with an adult chaperon present, but touching and hand-holding was not allowed. Young people sometimes dated behind their parents' backs, but this was risky as the consequences for getting caught by strict Italian parents could be quite harsh.

Young lovers who couldn't be together often wrote love notes to one another and had them delivered by a mutual friend or acquaintance. This kind of messaging would sometimes go on for months, even years.

These days, couples will sometimes date for several years before getting engaged. In fact dating in Italy and throughout the world has become more casual. Some people date more than one person at a time, while others date exclusively. Some date for fun, while others date in an effort to start a relationship. Many people do a lot of dating before finding that one special person, while others may have found that one special person in kindergarten and never do any dating at all.

The Italian Marriage Proposal

In the past, it had been customary for the prospective bride's father to be asked for permission to marry his daughter, and often it was someone other than the potential groom who did the asking. Typically, a male relative of the hopeful suitor would pay the girl's father (or uncle) a visit to discuss the possibility of marriage. Or sometimes a matchmaker or "masciata" would be sent to inform the girl's father about the boy's interest in marrying his daughter. Most of the time, when the proposal was made it was not the first the girl's parents knew about it.

Once the parents of the would-be bride and groom had agreed to the marriage, the young man would be given the go-ahead and he'd plan his official proposal, which was usually made to the young woman's parents. If he passed that test, it was time to propose to his beloved. Most of the time, the betrothed-to-be already knew she was going to be proposed to, but she didn't always know how or when it would happen.

Romance was essential in the young man's proposal to the young woman. He may have serenaded her, playing a musical instrument himself, or having some friends play instruments while he focused on the duty at hand: the asking. He might have written a song and sang it to her, regardless of his singing ability, or perhaps he would write her a love poem and recite it to her. The more creative he was in his romantic proposal, the better, although, for the most part, the young woman was dazzled just that he asked her to marry him.

The Diamond Engagement Ring

During his romantic proposal, the young Italian man might offer his sweetheart a token of his love and intent in the form of a diamond ring. According to Italian folklore, the diamond was believed to be produced by the flames of love, which was fitting to a situation in which a young man professed his true love. On a less romantic note, there is a practical component to the giving of a diamond ring. Frankly put, the diamond ring was seen as a symbol of the groom's "payment" for his bride: he must be serious in his intent to marry her if he is offering her such an expensive token of his love. In that spirit, it was widely believed that the bigger the diamond, the better. That he could afford such a rock showed the bride's family that he could offer their daughter financial security and be well able to support her and a family. A substantial diamond engagement ring significantly increased a young man's value as a future son-in-law and let the young woman know he must really love her.

A young woman with an exquisite diamond engagement ring on her finger was the envy of her friends. The ring represented the promise of a wonderful life. She would soon go from being a girl living in her parents' home to a woman living with her husband in their own home, and soon to be having children of her own. Once the engagement was official, it was time for the wedding planning to commence.

The Engagement Party

Sometimes instead of—or in addition to—proposing in private, a young man might ask his true love to marry him in front of his and her entire family and close friends. This was typically done at a party planned by the young woman's parents after the young man asked for their permission to marry their daughter, and held at her parents' house. It was customary for the whole family, even town, to be involved in this joyous event. People wanted to be present at this, the official beginning of the wedding process because a wedding was by far the biggest celebration there was. Engagement parties typically featured a large feast and music. Most of the guests already knew the purpose of the party, and came with gifts—usually monetary.

Both families contributed to the party. The bride's parents supplied their home, food, and hospitality. The groom's parents were often also involved. The young woman, who already knew what this night had in store for her, took the time to look as beautiful as ever. She also played co-hostess by greeting guests. But it was the young man who had the most demanding obligation. He had to prepare a speech to be delivered in front of dozens of bystanders as he "officially" proposed to his beloved. While he by this point had probably already been through two relatively painless proposals, now he had to come up with eloquence to dazzle the crowd, which was gathered there for the sole purpose of watching him propose. Understandably nervous, the young man would mingle with guests until his moment in the spotlight arrived.

At some point during the party, the young man, the young woman's father, or another male relative requested silence. The young man and young woman then took center stage as the guests gathered round. He began his speech, which was addressed to the young woman, her parents, and all of the guests, often starting out by politely addressing the young woman's parents, thanking them for their blessing, and then thanking the guests for coming. And then, the moment of truth: after warming everyone up with his salutations, he would turn to his sweetheart and deliver the speech he worked so long and hard to compose. She might then blush, perhaps cry tears of joy, and agree to marry him. The guests would cheer. Then someone would propose a toast and the festivities would begin again and the party generally lasted well into the night.

In another form of the engagement party, the proposal was already made and accepted, and the party was thrown to announce that the young couple had become engaged. Her father would make a speech welcoming him into the family, and guests would celebrate with the couple and share in their joy.

Once Engaged

Once the engagement became official, the next several months were a time of abundant activity. The wedding planning began and would continue right up to the very last minute before the wedding. Planning an elaborate Italian wedding took from six months to two years. The couple and their families were thrown into a busy whirl making sure that every detail was tended to.

It was joyous time for the many people involved. The young woman glowed with excitement in anticipation of her wedding day and starting her new life, and was showered with attention, wishes of good fortune, and material possessions. He also enjoyed his share of attention as older men offered him advice and he was also given many gifts.

In the next chapter, we'll delve into what takes place during the Italian wedding planning process, both then and now. For the rest of this chapter, let's explore the many ways that you can use Italian traditions in your engagement.

Italian Engagement Traditions

While many of old-world Italy's pre-wedding traditions seem antiquated now, certain aspects still translate to the modern wedding. Of course, if you're already planning your wedding, chances are you've already met your significant other, dated for a while, developed your relationship, and probably gotten engaged. However, there are still elements of these ancient traditions you can take to liven up this special time.

Involve Your Parents

As we know, family plays a significant role in Italian culture. While long ago, it was common and expected for a young man to get a girl's parents' permission to marry her, this doesn't happen very often today. It's more likely that your fiancé asked you to marry him, and then you told your parents. But that doesn't mean you can't include them in the process. Simply make it a point to include them as much as possible in the planning.

One thing that is customary is to introduce your parents to one another if they haven't already met. Set up an introductory parents dinner at a cozy Italian restaurant. This is a great time for you, your fiancé, and both sets of parents to discuss general plans about the upcoming wedding. In the comfortable setting of a favorite restaurant, the mood is light and everyone is at ease. Even if they have already met, this will give them an opportunity to talk prior to the wedding, which will make the wedding planning process run more smoothly.

Spend some time with your own parents. Let them know how much you love them and thank them for raising you. Go to dinner with your mom and dad and spend an afternoon with each of them individually.

Get to know his mom. Have him get to know your dad. Plan outings together. Maybe he, your dad, his dad, your brother, and any other close male relative could go fishing together. And you, your mom, his mom, and close female relatives could plan an outing together as well. His family are soon to be your in-laws, and if they're like most Italian families, there is going to be a lot of interaction till death do you part. This is a good time to get acquainted.

Recapture the Small-Town Magic

The way Italian couples met and ended up together in the old days had a lot to do with living in small towns and villages where everyone knew each other. You may or may not have grown up in a small town, but you probably have some concept of what that small-town feeling is. During your engagement, seek out a nearby small town with a charming "downtown" area with shops, restaurants, and cafés, and make it your place. Perhaps, you and your fiancé could celebrate your engagement together at a quaint restaurant there. Or you could spend some time alone during the upcoming months of planning browsing the shops, or getting lost in a book together at an outdoor café. You might even find some great shops in which to acquire some of your wedding items. You're sure to find a bridal boutique or bakery that has just what you're looking for. Look for places to find invitations, wedding favors, jewelry, or bridal party gifts. Or there might be a great little Italian restaurant perfect for that "meet the parents" night.

Enjoy Some Good Old-Fashioned Dating

Go on an old-fashioned Italian date with your fiancé. Long ago in Italy, unmarried people weren't allowed to date without a chaperone; however, some got around this by going out with a group of friends, while others would sneak off to see each other. For fun, why not plan one—or all—of these three kinds of old-fashioned Italian dates.

Plan a date with a chaperone. Go out together and take along a parent, grandparent, or other older relative. Of course, this will be less like having a chaperon there to keep an eye on you and more like including someone you care about in your outing.

If you plan a date with a group of friends, gather a group of fun couples and go out. Do something festive, childlike, or outrageous, like playing miniature golf, or visiting an amusement park or video arcade, or checking out a themed pizza parlor, interactive dinner or play, comedy club, or a concert. Or, gather up a bunch of your single friends and have him gather up some of his for a get-together. And who knows—perhaps a match might be made.

Or, for fun, pretend that this is old-time Italy, and that you have to see each other alone secretly. As the wedding date gets closer, this might actually become necessary as you'll both be pulled in so many different directions with the wedding planning process in full swing. The two of you will most likely want to break away from time to time to catch your breath and be alone together. Find a place you both like to go or an activity you enjoy doing together and make a point of "sneaking off" to it during the upcoming months. Make a list of your favorite "secret hideaways" and refer to it as needed. It may include simple suggestions like the corner coffee shop or your backyard patio or more provocative places like a weekend getaway in the mountains or at the beach. Whatever the case, it's nice to have something that is just the two of you together. This will be a practice you will want to hold on to throughout your marriage as well.

Another way young couples related in the old days was through written love notes. This is still a romantic and meaningful way of communicating in which you and your fiancé can participate. There is nothing more simple yet thoughtful than writing a sweet note from the heart and leaving it somewhere for your beloved to find—on his pillow, in his briefcase or sports bag, or on his doorstep, even in his mailbox. Write loving and romantic words on pretty stationery or pick up a sentimental greeting card from time to time. This is another practice to continue doing throughout your marriage.

Revisit Romantic Italian Proposals

Most likely, your sweetie has already proposed at this point. But you can still capture the essence of the old-fashioned Italian wedding proposal in other ways. Romantic proposals often feature an element of surprise, so focus on that and surprise your fiancé—for his birthday, for Valentine's Day, or just because—with a massage, a homemade candlelit dinner, by baking his favorite cookies, or with some other thoughtful gesture.

Many old-fashioned Italian wedding proposals featured a serenade. You could croon to your fiancé at a karaoke restaurant. Or you could learn a duet together. If you're serious and have the voice, you could even plan to sing this at the wedding. Otherwise, singing together might just be something fun to do on an evening out or at home.

Plan an Italian-style Engagement Party

Like in the old days, many couples hold engagement parties to celebrate. Today the purpose of such a party is to let everyone know that you are getting married and to possibly announce the wedding date. Your friends and relatives will want to congratulate you and share their joy and best wishes. This engagement party usually occurs after most friends and family members have already been told the good news. An engagement party can be as simple as a small dinner party at a home or restaurant, or as elaborate as a big party with lots of guests.

When planning an engagement party, decide approximately how many guests you want to invite and determine the best venue in which to accommodate this number. Remember, whomever you invite to the engagement party should also be invited to the wedding. However, you don't necessarily have to invite all the wedding guests to the engagement party; closest friends and relatives will suffice.

Plan your party for afternoon or evening on a Saturday or Sunday. It can include just drinks and appetizers, a full meal, or simply dessert and coffee. It can be a sitdown dinner or "eat-as-you-mingle." Whatever you do, allow enough time to plan the event, and book any caterers, entertainment, and other services you need well enough in advance. How long you need to plan this event will depend on many factors. I suggest that you don't spend so long planning the engagement party that it takes away from the wedding planning or that you wait too long after you are engaged to have it. Also send invitations out early. Three to four weeks prior to the event should be sufficient.

The parents of the bride still often host the engagement party. However, the groom's parents can host or help out as well, as can the bride and groom themselves.

An Engagement Party With "Old Time" Touches

You and your fiancé might host an old-fashioned Italian engagement party together. Invite both families and close friends. Serve Italian finger foods, such as antipasto, pan pizza, calamari, and mozzarella sticks along with Italian wines. For entertainment, hire a professional karaoke vendor to bring an entire karaoke system, with microphones, word screen, and a wide selection of songs. Here, you can incorporate a twist on the "romantic serenade" engagement tradition. At some point during the party, you and your fiancé take center stage for an announcement. Here you can honor your parents by making a toast to each. Perhaps you can hold a wine tasting party, hire a string quartet, plan an auction, play games such as a matchmaking game with single guests or a "Who Knows this Couple Best?" game with all. The engagement party is also a great time to announce the bridal party.

Or try planning a "surprise" engagement party, at which you announce your engagement to your unsuspecting guests. Invite guests over for a dinner party—complete with huge Italian meal, Italian love songs playing—and when the moment comes to break the good news, play the traditional wedding march or Italian wedding song (see chapter 10). You can insert little notes (like fortunes) in canollis that announce your engagement, hire a singing telegram to serenade your guests with the news (this can be an opera singer or Frank Sinatra, Pavarotti, or other singer impersonator), hire a trumpet player and have someone read the announcement from a scroll, or have souvenirs that guests can keep as mementos. These might be goblets—engraved with your announcement—such as "John and Sue became engaged on September 2, 2002."

Engagement Announcements

Another way to announce your engagement is by putting it in print. Send out your own announcements to everyone you know. This can also be a "save-the-date" notice, letting people post your wedding date on their calendar long before the invitations go out.

Many newspapers run some type of engagement and wedding announcements. Check with your local newspaper for their policies. These announcements are often run with a photo, so if you plan to have official engagement photos taken, get started on that right away. Or you may already have a favorite picture of you and your fiancé that you want to use. Make sure you allow enough time for the engagement announcement to run. Newspapers often have a backlog of as much as two or three months.

Once you're engaged and everyone knows about it, you can get to the real fun: planning your Italian wedding.

5

Wedding Planning Process

PLANNING A WEDDING, WHETHER it be an all-out Italian production, or even a small and subtle affair, takes a lot of time and organization. It is important to determine what is involved, who does what, and how long everything takes to get done.

Anyone who has planned a wedding can tell you it's no small task. But most will tell you that the process itself can be an enjoyable experience that you will never forget.

Italian Wedding Planning in the Past

Once an Italian couple became engaged and the engagement was announced, they immediately started planning for the big day. Their parents, especially the bride's parents, played a big role in this planning process, from the funding of the elaborate wedding celebration to how and where the couple would live after they were married.

For the bride's parents, much of the preparation for their daughter's wedding day had taken place ever since she was a young girl, sometimes since her birth. They started a "trousseau" or dowry for her, to which they added items over the years. It often consisted of monetary savings, which would be spent on the extravagant wedding celebration, as well as money for the couple's home, and everything she would need for the home once she was married.

The Italian Trousseau

The trousseau, also known as a "dote" or hope chest, holds a collection of marriage supplies. It consisted of housewares, such as kitchenware, china, linens, and other household items. Through the years, the eventual bride received these treasures as gifts for birthdays and other occasions. And once she was engaged, her parents would throw in anything that she still needed. This included her clothing and sometimes even her future husband's clothing. During the wedding planning process, the bride assembled these items, and got them ready to bring to their new home.

Long ago, these trousseaus were often very carefully packed and left in special hiding places as there had been many wars in Italy; the hiding was done in an effort to conceal these valuable items from soldiers of an invading army who might steal them.

Today, many brides-to-be in many cultures assemble hope chests. Through the years they collect beautiful items for their future homes. Parents and relatives might buy for her an expensive and exquisite piece of crystal or china here and there. Before she knows it, she has amassed quite a collection and has a nice head start on things for her home.

These days, however, many women acquire household items as they are away at college, or while living on their own before getting married. In this case, a hope chest isn't a necessity because the women are actually already using their household items. However, they might acquire certain valuable pieces that they'll put away for when they get married.

Italian Bridal Showers

Some say bridal showers have not always been an Italian wedding tradition, that the tradition has evolved in more recent years. This is because in the old days in Italy, the bride-to-be already had all of her household items from her trousseau and therefore a bridal shower would not be necessary. Others claim that bridal showers have long been customary at least in some parts of Italy and that at traditional Italian bridal showers, the bride-to-be received money and household items from friends and relatives.

Today, bridal showers are a big part of Italian weddings. This is especially true now that most women don't grow up with such an elaborate collection of household items. The bridal shower is a great way to start a modern-day trousseau. And it allows the future bride to spend some time with her family and friends and her future husbands' female relatives. Most bridal showers are hosted by a female relative or friend of the bride-to-be, are held on a Saturday or Sunday afternoon, and feature refreshments. Sometimes games are played, and often the bride-to-be opens her gifts in front of guests. Gifts nowadays can be just about anything, from housewares to personal items. In chapter 12, "Unique Italian Touches," we will discuss unique ideas for adding Italian touches to your bridal shower.

Bridal Registry

Long ago, the items that went into a young woman's trousseau were often those that had been passed down from her ancestors or gifts chosen by the giver. These days, many couples choose their own gifts through a bridal registry. Many department stores offer gift registries for couples to choose their own household goods, including pots, pans, knives, appliances, everyday dishes and glasses, silverware, fine china, crystal, towels, bathroom accessories, bedding, and even luggage, picture frames, furniture, and electronics. Nowadays you can register for just about anything. And many couples register at two or three different stores, covering all the basics and beyond and giving people a wide variety of gift buying options.

Here are some hints for registering for wedding gifts. First, make sure you register enough ahead of time. You don't want to be rushed when picking out all your treasures. Often, more than one day is required for registering, especially if you're planning on registering at more than one store. And while it may seem like a lot of fun to zap everything your heart desires with the scanner gun, it can also be overwhelming. Shopping around before you actually register is a very good idea. If your husband-to-be hates shopping and does not care which silverware pattern goes well with what china pattern, save both of you the grief and bring your mother, sister, or a willing friend instead. Or go twice—once with him to pick out the "fun" stuff, like knife sets and appliances, and once again for everything else. It's also a good idea to call the store first and find out if an appointment is necessary.

After you've registered, give your shower hostess all the information so she can inform guests ahead of time. While it is standard practice to include bridal registry information in the shower invitation, it isn't necessary to include it in your wedding invitation. In fact, word of mouth works best.

The bridal registry is a common practice these days and can be a convenient way for couples to receive gifts they prefer, reducing the chance of receiving ten toasters and four blenders but no coffeemaker, and giving guests who have no idea what to buy some direction. However, some people will want the option of giving you something they choose. How else can Aunt Sophie bestow upon you that fine Italian silver that has been in the family for ages? And very likely, many guests, especially older ones, will want to give you good old-fashioned cash.

The Italian Bride and Groom's New Home

Another common wedding planning consideration in the old days was where the young couple would live once they were married. In Southern Italy, it was customary for the bride's parents to either buy or build the young couple a home. This home was usually near the bride's parents' home and was sometimes nicer than their own home. When building the couple's home, the parents would begin as soon as the couple became engaged and the home was often completed by the time of the wedding, a year or so later.

Sometimes the couple would live in the parents' back house or they would inherit the parents' home. Italian families always stayed close together and interacted on a regular basis. The young couple's parents helped with new babies, and couples took care of elderly parents. Today many Italian families throughout the world keep these close bonds. In some parts of Italy the living arrangements of couples about to be married are still influenced by where the parents live. However, it isn't as common for parents to buy or build the couple's home.

As the bride's family was responsible for providing the shelter, the groom would supply all the furniture for the home. This meant that he would choose what he liked and arrange it in the home. The bride would eventually bring in all the linen—sheets, tablecloths, and bedding—and other household items.

Where modern couples plan to live after they are married depends on many factors. They may or may not already live together before they are married, one may already own a home and the other might move in, or they might start shopping for a home together once they are engaged and move in to it after the wedding. Some might even live with parents for a while after they are married in order to save for a home. Also, the parents of either the bride or the groom—or both—may help with the purchase of a new home.

Bachelor and Bachelorette Parties

The custom of having a bachelor party is not one of the well-known Italian wedding traditions. While some people say it has always been customary for men to get together for "stag" parties prior to the wedding, others say that this trend didn't always exist in Italy. And, in Southern Italy, it is quite uncommon.

In modern times, however, men and women of many different cultures celebrate that "last" night or weekend with their same-sex friends. Bachelor and bachelorette parties can consist of anything from a simple dinner party with friends, an evening out, a daylong fishing trip, or sporting event to a weekend trip to Las Vegas, Miami Beach, or New Orleans. Some couples might even have a group pre-party with men and women to celebrate the upcoming wedding. While you're enjoying all of this pre-celebration celebrating, you still have to keep all of the various wedding balls in the air. The next section will take a close look at all of the elements you need to worry about to create a successful wedding, and provide you with guidance for each.

Wedding Planning Basics

When it comes to planning your Italian wedding, there are a few things you need to know before you even begin to think of anything else: where, when, how many, and how much. Where, when, and how many are interdependent and therefore need to be decided at the same time. Of course, the budget you have for your wedding will have a huge impact on these three factors.

Where to Hold Your Italian Wedding

Where you choose to hold your wedding—the ceremony and reception—sets the tone for everything else. In the old days, Italian wedding ceremonies were held at the nearest Catholic church, which was often where the bride and groom had grown up going to church and even attending Catholic school. The priest who married them probably had known them since they were children. There was no question about where they'd be married and who would perform the ceremony. As for the wedding reception, it was held either at the bride's or groom's parents' home or at a local banquet room.

Today, brides and grooms have many more choices about where to hold their weddings. While a truly traditional Italian wedding ceremony is held in a Catholic church, it doesn't have to be. And a wedding reception can be held anywhere that can accommodate the number of guests you plan to invite. Consider places that will best enhance your Italian wedding theme when choosing your wedding ceremony and reception sites. And make sure you book it far enough in advance. You may need to give up to a year or year and a half advance notice for some locations—and sometimes more. The time of year may also affect the wedding locations' availability.

When to Hold Your Italian Wedding

Time of year is a big wedding planning consideration. Not only does time of year affect your location choice (and vice versa), but it also sets the tone for everything from wedding wardrobe to flowers and decorations. An outdoor wedding is more practical in June than December; bridesmaids in black velvet look stunning on a February evening but awkward on a sunny August afternoon in a garden.

Before choosing your location, you may have a general idea about when you'd like your wedding to be, but you may pinpoint the exact date once you choose your wedding sites. And while you may have a sense of exactly what time of day you want for your wedding, the availability of the church and the banquet hall might decide what time the ceremony and reception begin.

How Many Guests to Invite

Another major wedding consideration is the approximate number of guests you wish to invite. This number can range from two to a thousand. Italian weddings have traditionally been on the larger side, averaging from about two hundred to six hundred guests. In the old days, whole towns would be invited to Italian weddings. In more recent times, guests consist of friends and relatives, which can seem like entire towns. You'll need to decide early on the size of the guest list, and this means talking to your fiancé, your parents, and his parents and coming to an early agreement. This might also mean that everyone needs to make a list of those people they absolutely must invite.

You may end up with four lists, some longer than others. If the numbers seem reasonable, you're lucky. Your wedding reception location may very well have a limit as to how many guests you can invite. If this limit is too small to accommodate your number, you'll have to decide whether it's more important for you to have your celebration at that location and invite less guests or to invite as many guests as you had planned and choose another location.

Your Italian Wedding Budget

For some, paying for a wedding is not a big concern. In the past, Italian parents often had a lot of money put away for their daughter's wedding. It was expected of them. These days, this isn't the norm for most people, and, therefore, the wedding budget is important. And unlike the old days, when the young woman's parents paid for the entire wedding, today the groom's parents often assist with the wedding costs, and, in many cases, the bride and groom themselves pitch in as well, or sometimes pay for the entire wedding themselves.

Once you have established your wedding budget—whether the sky's the limit or if there is only a certain amount of money you can spend—and who is going to pay for what, you will have some more guidelines to help you in many of your wedding planning decisions. Your budget will determine the other three initial considerations: Some locations cost more than others, certain times of the year and times during the day cost more than others, and the more guests you invite, the more money you're going to spend.

Once you're able to coordinate budget, location, date and time, and the number of guests, you will have accomplished a major wedding planning feat. From here on out, the rest is fun.

Planning Calendar

Planning a wedding, especially an elaborate Italian wedding, can be a time-consuming process. How much time you need to plan your wedding depends on many factors. First of all, it depends on you. How much time do you have? Do you work part-time or full-time, go to school, have many other commitments? If you are extremely busy, are you very organized and energetic and thrive on lots of projects going on at once? Also, who will be involved in the wedding planning process—just you, or will your fiancé, your parents, his parents, relatives, friends, a wedding coordinator also take part? And who will be doing what? These are things you'll need to consider in the early stages of your wedding planning process.

Planning a wedding takes organization. You will be tending to lots of details so you'll need some kind of organizational system. If you've already set the date and booked your locations for the ceremony and reception, you now have a time frame in which to work. You will need a wedding planning calendar and a notebook for keeping all of your wedding planning materials together. Let's say your wedding is ten months from now. Make a list of all of the wedding planning activities you will need to be involved in from now until then. Then, get your wedding calendar and plot all of the things that must take place at a certain time before the wedding. For example, invitations should go out two months before the wedding, so eight months from now plan to send invitations out. Then, go two months ahead of that and write in "choose wedding invitations." Many wedding planning guides and wedding magazines feature wedding planning timelines of planning aspects to take care of nine to twelve months before the wedding and all the way up to the day of the wedding. Use these as a guide to fill in your wedding planning calendar.

If this all seems too much for you, consider hiring a professional wedding planner. You might want to consider this if you are weighed down with numerous commitments, or you don't have a lot of help, time, patience, or resources that you feel are necessary for planning the Italian wedding of your dreams. Or you may just want an extra pair of hands to carry out some of the details. An established wedding planner has a wealth of contacts in the industry and can help you to find great florists, caterers, photographers, and so on.

Choosing Vendors

During your wedding planning, you will likely be looking for talented and reputable help in many areas. There are several ways to go about finding the right vendors. Just make sure that you: (a) see, hear, taste, or sample their work in some way; and (b) get a written, signed contract.

How do you find good wedding help? A good way is through word of mouth. Talk to couples who got married recently and find out who they hired and what they thought of their services. Otherwise, check the yellow pages and wedding publications and start calling around. Ask lots of questions, starting with whether or not they are booked on the date of your wedding, and make an appointment to meet each vendor in person to see their work. Compare and contrast everything you find out, and make the best choice based on the information you receive. Following are the main vendors you will be evaluating for your Italian wedding.

Caterer Once you have secured your location, date, and time, your first priority is to find a caterer. Food is very important, and at an Italian wedding, it is extremely so. Deciding who to hire to feed your guests is a major decision and one that should be considered with care. We will talk more about hiring an Italian food caterer in chapter 9, when we discuss Italian wedding food in depth. Some reception locations provide their own catering. If so, you will need to find out if your reception site provides the kind of food you want, and if not, whether or not you can bring in an outside caterer.

Photographer A good photographer is very important, and good ones often get booked early. So, you will probably want to start scouting out photographers right away. If you know a couple who was married not too long ago, ask if you can look at their wedding pictures and find out what it was like working with that photographer. When you meet with the photographer, make sure you look at as many samples of her work as possible, and get a price quote in writing.

Videographer Much like the photographer, a videographer captures your wedding day forever, and can have a serious impact on how those memories are stored. Having a video of your wedding day in addition to your photographs is very important. In addition to catching the visuals, a good video captures the entire atmosphere—the music, the energy, the comments made by your loved ones. When you meet with potential videographers, be sure to see a sample of their work. This may mean having to sit through the wedding videos of people you don't know, but it will be worth it in the long run when you pop in that tape and relive your Italian wedding in the years to come.

Florist The one who brings flowers brings life to your Italian wedding, and therefore the role of the florist is crucial. Look for someone who is creative and who has a vision of her own, yet will listen to you and work with your vision. Look at photos of her work and ask lots of questions. Let the florist know that you are planning an Italian wedding, and everything else you know at that point—the location, time of year, and color scheme if you've decided—and ask for ideas and suggestions. Bring photographs of your wedding sites so the florist has visuals to work with. Set a date for the florist to visit the wedding site prior to the wedding so she can see exactly what it looks like. In addition to enhancing your wedding site, the florist will be preparing your bouquet and all of the personal flowers—the bridesmaids' bouquets, mothers' corsages, men's boutonnieres. The floral decorations will enhance the overall look, so you want to make sure you hire the best.

Bridal Gown The next wedding planning step is finding the perfect wedding gown. This might take some time, so you'll want to start looking early on. In fact many bridal shops require four to six months to order a gown. And then you'll need to schedule at least two more fittings prior to the wedding.

Band or DJ The music at your Italian wedding is very important. The music also works to set the mood and is the focus of the entertainment for the event. We will discuss hiring bands, DJs, and musicians in detail in chapter 10, when talking about music for your Italian wedding. Just make sure you start looking for your music providers early on.

Transportation How you and your bridal party get to and from the wedding is an important consideration. Most couples rent limousines for their wedding transportation. You'll need to find out how far in advance you need to book a limo in your area and proceed accordingly.

Invitations As mentioned, wedding invitations should be mailed out about two months before the wedding, and they need to be ordered a couple of months before that. Playing it safe would mean that you start looking at wedding invitations about six months before the wedding. You may have to go to several places before you find what you're looking for. As far as Italian wedding invitations go, it may take even longer to find something you like or for someone to custom design what you want. Remember that your wedding invitation is the first thing about your wedding that people see—except for maybe an engagement announcement or save-the-date notice—and it gives them an idea of what's to come. An invitation with an Italian flair is a great Italian wedding opener.

Bridesmaids' Dresses   Once you've decided on your color scheme, you and your bridesmaids will want to start shopping for bridesmaids' dresses. This may or may not be at the same place where you bought your wedding gown. You will want to take your bridesmaids' preferences into consideration as well as price. Make sure the gowns are ordered in time, as they, too, can take a month or longer to make, and then may need extra time for alterations.

Wedding Cake   The wedding cake can be a very important part of a wedding celebration, and many couples want to be sure that they order the perfect cake that reflects their tastes—both in how it tastes and how it looks. Wedding cakes come in every flavor, size, and style, so you'll probably want to shop around at different bakeries, tasting samples and viewing photographs.

Favors   Sometimes deciding what to give your guests as a thank you for attending your wedding isn't easy. You need to come up with two hundred or so of the same little trinket that doesn't cost much but still makes a statement. And some, as we will discuss later, require some assembly. Make sure you schedule adequate time for shopping for and preparing your wedding favors.

Wedding Accessories   Guest books and pens, flower girl baskets, wedding cake knives, unity candles, and other specialized wedding items are also needed. You will want to shop around a bit for these accessories, which may have to be ordered. Make sure you allow enough time for delays or wrong orders.

Bridal Hair and Makeup Don't wait until the last minute to look for a good hairdresser and makeup artist for your wedding day. You'll want to book these resources early. And before the actual wedding day, you'll want a trial hair and makeup run to make sure you're not in for a surprise on your wedding day.

Honeymoon If you're planning to take a honeymoon, it's never too soon to start researching. Depending on where you plan to go, you may want to consider using a travel agent to help plan. As always, shop around, ask lots of questions, and give yourselves plenty of time to decide on what you want. Another option is to research honeymoon destinations on the Internet. Often, the earlier you book your reservations, the better deal you can get. And if you're traveling abroad, you'll need a passport if you don't already have one. If you do have one, make sure it has not expired—or will not expire before you need to use it.

Wedding Rings Shopping for wedding rings can be time consuming. You may know ahead of time what you want, or you may have no idea. If you're having rings designed or created, you'll need to allow more time, also, allow time for ring sizing.

Tuxedos You will need to pick out tuxedos (or suits) for the groom and the groomsmen. You will want to start shopping for the place that offers exactly what you're looking for and start setting dates for fittings. Make sure you find a place that has a reputation for being reliable.

Wedding Programs A wedding program is a nice touch to a wedding celebration, informing the guests of who is in the bridal party, the titles of certain songs and readings, and the significance of various wedding traditions that take place throughout the wedding. Make sure you allow enough time for yourself or someone else to design the program, choose the paper, and have it printed. You will also need to consider the program's assembly. Using ribbon or tassels may be a nicer touch than glue or staples.

Thank Yous Thank you notes are sometimes included in the wedding invitation package, but when they are not, make sure you purchase thank you notes and start sending them out as soon as you begin receiving wedding gifts.

Bridal Party Gifts It is a nice gesture to thank those people who serve as your bridesmaids, groomsmen, flower girls, ring bearers, and so on. Giving them a thoughtful gift is a great way to let them know you appreciate them. Take the time to find the perfect gifts. It is more practical to give them each the same gift, which can be monogrammed for a personal touch, although you can also buy them each something that reflects their individual tastes. Finding personal gifts takes time, and it's not something you want to save for the last minute and risk buying something inappropriate. Plus, having gifts engraved takes extra time.

Miscellaneous Items Decorative items and props that are not part of the floral arrangements, including vases, fabric, tulle, ribbon, linens, and other elements that you add to the wedding décor, will need to be purchased in advance. Allow enough time for items that need to be ordered and/or delivered.

Special Considerations for Home Weddings

If you decide to hold a wedding at home—yours, your parents', or the home of a friend or relative—there are even more essentials to tend to. You will need to find a great rental company. Shop around for one that offers the best equipment at the best prices. Make sure that the items you need are available when you need them and that they are in good condition. Most rental companies will deliver your rentals the day before the wedding and pick them up the day after. Insist on a written contract. The following are some of the items you may need to rent for an at-home wedding: dinner, cocktail, gift, cake, and food tables, chairs, umbrellas, tent, dance floor, altar, tablecloths, napkins, cooking and serving ware—if not provided by caterer—plates, silverware, glassware, salt and pepper shakers, coffeemakers and servers, coffee cups, cream and sugar holders, bars, stages and platforms, and microphone and speaker systems.

In addition, having a home wedding might require you to acquire extra bathrooms, depending on the number of guests. There are companies that rent portable bathrooms, complete with lighting, running water, sinks, and mirrors.

Another important consideration is whether there will be enough electricity to sustain extra lighting and sound systems. Call a trusted electrician to visit the property ahead of time and assess the electricity available. You will probably have to ask your DJ or band what their electricity requirements are. You can have more power brought in as needed to accommodate the special needs for the day, and eliminate power failure.

You will also need to consider how beverages will be served at your wedding. Unless your caterer provides bar service, you may need to hire one or more bartenders to pour drinks. You will also need to decide what types of drinks you will serve and order them in advance.

When holding a wedding at a home, you may need to hire extra help to keep things running smoothly, to help the caterers serve food and drinks, to keep the bathrooms clean and stocked, to dispose of garbage and empty trash cans, to move chairs from the wedding ceremony area to the dinner tables, and various other things that are usually taken care of automatically at banquet halls.

Wedding Rehearsal and Rehearsal Dinner

In the old days in Italy, there were no wedding rehearsals. Everyone showed up on the day of the wedding and did their part. Today it is common to have a wedding rehearsal a day or two before the wedding. In fact, many churches require the bride, groom, and wedding party to take part in a practice run of the wedding ceremony to eliminate confusion on the day of the wedding. This way everyone knows where to stand and what to do during the wedding ceremony.

The Catholic wedding ceremony has many rituals, and the bride and groom are required to move around the altar during various parts. During the rehearsal, they run through the ceremony positions several times, sometimes with the music.

A rehearsal dinner for the bridal party, close relatives, and out-of-town guests often follows the rehearsal. This is a chance for everyone to mingle and celebrate prior to the wedding day, when there might not be a chance to spend as much time with loved ones. The rehearsal dinner is usually held at a nice restaurant, and is customarily paid for by the groom's parents.

Of course there are variations of rehearsals and dinners. For simpler wedding ceremonies, a rehearsal might not be necessary. Some rehearsal dinners are much more casual get-togethers, such as a pizza party at someone's home.

More Wedding Planning Considerations

If you are going to have a Catholic wedding ceremony, you will be required to attend a marriage counseling "pre-cana" program. This often consists of several meetings with the priest and a weekend "engagement encounter." Once you choose your wedding ceremony location, talk to your priest about these requirements and possible dates.

Other wedding planning criteria to start thinking about include: what style or formality you would like for your wedding; the season of year in which it takes place and what the weather will be like at that time; what to you are the most important wedding elements; and other cultural customs and/or wedding themes you will incorporate into your wedding.

These are some of the main components that go into the planning of a wedding of any type. During your Italian wedding planning, you will most likely need to contact venues and vendors to provide these places, products, and services. Just make sure you allow enough time to scout out the best. Meanwhile you can focus on incorporating Italian traditions and touches to your wedding.

The key is to plan ahead and plan some more. Don't assume anything. If you don't make the necessary arrangements, it likely won't happen. Remember that an Italian wedding is a very special event that can be quite elaborate and therefore time-consuming in its planning. Think of it as a major production, your own little Italian movie, in which you write the script, scout the location, choose the cast and crew, direct, produce, and launch the premiere. Tend to every tedious detail. It's the details that make for a spectacular event.

Location Suggestions for Italian Wedding Ceremonies and Receptions

- church
- dock
- ship
- office building
- motel
- winery
- forest
- barn
- castle
- theater
- greenhouse

- chapel
- cliff
- bridge
- historic site
- banquet hall
- brewery
- beach
- museum
- villa
- courtyard
- opera house

- vineyard
- monastery
- cathedral
- historic house
- warehouse
- garden
- farm
- gallery
- cottage
- hot-air balloon
- library

- courthouse
- boat
- landmark
- hotel
- restaurant
- open field
- desert
- park
- movie set
- amusement park
- lighthouse

6

Italian Wedding Wardrobe

WHAT DO BRIDES, GROOMS, and others typically wear during and leading up to the Italian wedding? How do you choose the right bridal gown, bridesmaids' dresses, suits and tuxes, shoes, and accessories all with an Italian flair? Let's explore some of the aspects involved in the Italian wedding wardrobe.

What you wear on your wedding day plays an important role in the overall success of your Italian wedding. And every detail counts—your gown, veil, shoes, accessories, hair, makeup, and not to mention what the groom and bridal party wear and the flowers you choose to be carried and worn.

Many of the aspects related to your Italian wedding wardrobe are influenced by Italian wedding traditions, some originated in ancient times, and others modern.

Italians and Looking Good

Italians have often been recognized for their attention to appearance. It has been said that in Italy, people often act as if they are on show. This might be because they spend so much time out in the piazzas and the streets. As a result, people are often judged more on their outward appearances than anything else. In many ways Italians have become accustomed to being on stage, performing grand productions in everything they do—speaking, eating, shopping, and just moving about.

Italians like to be on display and aim to look their best. Just look at all the attractive celebrities of Italian descent.

Famous Italian Beauties

🌀 Anne Bancroft
🌀 Valerie Bertinelli
🌀 Carla Bruni (model)
🌀 Madonna (Ciccone)
🌀 Linda Evangelista
🌀 Annette Funicello
🌀 Rita Hayworth (Margarita Cansino)
🌀 Tea Leoni (Pantleoni)
🌀 Sophia Loren
🌀 Alyssa Milano
🌀 Liza Minnelli
🌀 Isabella Rossellini
🌀 Christina Ricci
🌀 Annabella Sciorra
🌀 Mira Sorvino
🌀 Marisa Tomei

Famous Italian Hunks

🌀 Antonio Sabato, Jr.
🌀 John Travolta
🌀 Frank Sinatra
🌀 Frankie Valli
🌀 Leonardo DiCaprio
🌀 Rudolph Valentino

So when it comes to appearance, Italians have it mastered, which comes out in their landscapes, architecture, décor, arts, cooking, movies, celebrations, festivals, jewelry, fashion, and more.

Italians are often nicely dressed in the latest fashions and have a taste for the finer clothing. Italian women spend hours getting ready before going out, making sure their clothes, hair, and makeup are perfect.

Consider emulating some of their looks—makeup, hair, clothing style—for your wedding day look.

Italians and Fashion

Attention to appearance can be seen in the work of the many talented Italian fashion designers. In fact, what city is the fashion capital of the world? Not Paris or New York, but Italy's own Milan. A semi-annual fashion trade fair takes place in Milan, where Italian designers showcase their latest creations. Buyers come from all over the world to see and purchase from these spectacular collections.

Italian fashion design has become an art form in itself, taking color, fabric, stitching, construction, and design to new levels. The top fashion designers have reached artist and celebrity status.

The Italian people have grown accustomed to having exquisitely designed clothing, and take fashion very seriously. Italian women want the latest styles, the highest quality, and they want to be the first wearing it. It is not uncommon for an Italian woman to buy a whole new wardrobe each season, entirely discarding the one from the last.

And just like the Italian fashion designer, the Italian seamstress plays an important role. Also very talented, seamstresses are well known for their high-quality work and ability to make the customer look good. Many are able to tailor dresses to enhance a woman's figure—covering flaws and accentuating attributes.

Because of all this attention to detail in appearance and fashion, it is no wonder that bridal beauty and fashion plays such an important role in Italian weddings.

Many of the best fashion designers come from all over Italy, and lead the way with each season's fashions. Some of the top Italian designers and clothing brands include:

- Gucci
- Dolce & Gabbana
- Sergio Tacchini
- Studiomoda
- Xenia
- Piero Guidi
- Navy & Navy
- Mantero
- Lorenzi
- Magnificio
- Scaglione
- Laura Biagiotti
- Versace
- Armani
- Alfred Angelo

Before the Wedding

In the past, Italian brides-to-be made a point to wear green on the night before their weddings. The Italian bride-to-be may wear a splash or a full wash of the color, either to the evening before's activities or to sleep that night. It was believed that wearing green would bring luck and abundance to the bride and groom. While certain colors carry different meanings in various cultures, the color green is almost universally associated with good fortune. It is considered calming and refreshing, and is often associated with nature. It is also used as a symbol of money, peace and stability, hope, fertility, growth and abundance, external life, harmony, the month of March, youth, ambition, and progression.

If you want to incorporate the "green" tradition into your Italian wedding, consider wearing an item of clothing—dress, suit, sweater, blouse, or scarf—in any number of shades of green on the night before your wedding, to the rehearsal dinner, or to a quiet meal with family. Green comes in a variety of hues—forest, emerald, sea foam, mint, sage, olive, khaki, turquoise, and so on—so there's a shade of green that can appeal to anyone's particular tastes or preferences. Consider adding a hint of the color in a piece of jewelry, such as emerald or jade, or wear green undergarments or nightwear.

Italian Brides Wear White

Perhaps the single most important item of clothing an Italian girl will ever own will be her wedding gown. In Italy, the bride's dress was always white, never off-white or ivory. The color white has been a symbol of joyous celebration since ancient times. It has long been the symbol of purity and virginity. According to some Italians, if a bride wore ivory on her wedding day, it meant she had had a boyfriend and therefore was not pure.

Wedding Gown Styles

Some of the world's most regal wedding gowns are made in Italy. Annual bridal shows are held in Naples, where some of the finest silk and lace originates. Italian bridal gowns are often original and singular creations that feature the finest textiles and quality workmanship.

There are several designers and boutiques throughout the United States and in Italy that carry or specialize in Italian wedding gown designs. Here is a brief list; search the Internet (key words: Italian Wedding Gowns/Bridal Gowns) for more:

Sogno di Sposa
Handmade wedding gowns from dressmakers in Florence. Call
    or order online.
Tel: 39 055 715384
www.mayano.com/sposa

Vanni Chiacchierino
Italian wedding dresses and gowns for wholesalers, retailers,
    and prospective brides. Worldwide shipping available.
Tel: 39 080 405823
www.vannbride.com

Bridal Couture Italia
Italian wedding gown collection made to order in Venice. Fine
    fabrics decorated with Swarovski crystal, lace, and pearls.
www.bridalitalia.com
email: *bridalitalia@supanet.com*

Peter Langner
Italian designer in Rome. Gowns are available at bridal shops
    throughout the United States.
Tel: 39 068 078228
www.peterlangner.com

In the earliest Italian weddings, bridal gowns were often simple, long, and flowing, with modest enhancements and very short trains, if any. Through the years, the Italian wedding dress has become more elaborate with an assortment of bodice styles, possibly bedecked with glittery jewels; and perhaps having full billowy skirts and trains that extend several feet behind the dress. They come in a full range of styles and cuts, with a multitude of options for sleeves, fabrics, necklines, and accents. Some Italian wedding gowns are very ornate and romantic, made from rich fabrics like silk, organza, and lace, and enhanced with intricate detailing, brocade designs, crystal beads, and pearls.

Choosing Your Bridal Gown

When selecting the gown for your Italian wedding, you'll have many details to consider: the date, time, location, style, and formality of your wedding; your own personal style and preferences; comfort; the "look" you're after; price range; availability; and proximity of the bridal shop and/or seamstress. You may already know whether you prefer a traditional look—white dress, tight bodice, full skirt, and long train—or something more contemporary or casual. Following you will find some features of bridal gowns you'll need to think about before you decide what your perfect gown will be like.

Fabrics Brocade; satin, including silk Duchesse satin, polyester Duchesse satin, polyester satin, acetate satin, slipper satin; peau de soie; lace, including elaborate lace, antique lace, Venice lace, Chantilly lace, Wedgwood, embroidered net, Alençon, all over, Cluny, coin dot, re-embroidered, Schiffli, Valenciennes, cotton lace, or eyelet; heavy or light crepe; chiffon; organdy; taffeta; silks, including silk shantungs or Dupionis; velvet, including sueded velvet or cut velvet; sheers, including organza, silk satin organza, chiffon, tulle, tullonet; dotted Swiss; faille; moire; point d'esprit; batiste; polynet; lawn; knits.

Trims Beads; rhinestones; pearls; sequins; lace; appliques; insertions and edgings; pleated and ruffled trims; hand embroidery; eyelet; ribbon; metallics; fur; feathers.

Styles   Classic, A–line, or princess (for formal and semi-formal weddings); these gowns feature a slim, flowing silhouette, usually with long sleeves and a long train. Romantic or ball gown (for formal and semi-formal weddings); these feature a full skirt, with or without a train, often with tiers and/or ruffles, low and/or shaped neckline, puffy or capped sleeves; Garden (for semi-formal to informal weddings, indoors or outdoors); these feature soft fullness, delicate detailing such as tucks and embroidery, short, long, or no sleeves. Contemporary (for semi-formal to informal weddings); these gowns are simple, soft, fluid silhouettes, floor or street-length, one- or two-piece or sheath.

Lengths   Street just covers the knees; intermission hits between knees and ankles; ballet goes to the ankles; floor touches the floor; high-low is shorter in front and longer in back.

Trains   Brush is a couple of inches, which brush the floor; sweep can be up to six inches, sweeps the floor; chapel train extends one to three feet on the floor; semi-cathedral train extends four to five feet along the floor; cathedral train extends six to eight feet along the floor; extended or royal train extends ten feet or more along the floor; detachable train attaches to the waist by buttons, snaps or other method; Watteau train attaches at the shoulders/upper back, rather than at the waist.

Sleeves   Bishop, capped, dolman, gigot, illusion, melon, Renaissance, short, tapered, three-quarter, puffed, fitted, tunnel.

Necklines   Queen Anne, bateau, contessa, halter, illusion, high-neck, off-the-shoulder, portrait, sabrina, scoop, square, sweetheart, sweetheart back yoke, jewel, tank, V-neck, wedding band, open.

Waistline   Empire, natural, drop, basque, curved basque, dropped basque, asymmetrical.

When you begin shopping for your wedding gown, make sure to go with a positive attitude and plenty of time to spare. Taking your mother or a friend whose advice you respect is often helpful for a second opinion. But remember, don't be talked into a dress you're unsure of. You'll most likely just know which dress is "the one," whether it's the first dress you try on or the twenty-fifth. It will speak to you, as it complements your features, is comfortable, and makes you feel as beautiful as an Italian bride should.

Remember, your bridal gown will set the tone for your entire wedding, with everyone else following your lead for formality. As such, the Italian wedding gown shopping adventure is an event in itself. Have fun with it!

The Italian Wedding Veil

Once you've chosen the perfect wedding gown, you'll want to accessorize. And from Italian weddings long ago to the present day, the most important accessory has been the veil.

In Italian weddings, the bride always wore a veil, which was a prominent wedding feature even before the wedding dress became a staple. The veil, which was red in ancient Rome, was often quite long and served as the train.

Some say the veil represented virginity and innocence. Others say it can be traced back to ancient Roman times when the veil completely covered the bride from head to toe because the ancients believed that jealous evil spirits would try to cast a spell on a bride on her wedding day. So they would cover the bride with a veil to keep the evil spirits from harming her. Another belief is that the veil stems from the days when the groom would throw a blanket over a woman he wanted to marry and carry her away.

The wedding veil is believed to represent many things, including modesty, obedience, chastity, and youth. And for many brides today, the wedding veil plays a major part of the wedding tradition.

Choosing Your Wedding Veil

When choosing your wedding veil, there are various lengths to consider. Some veils reach to the shoulder, elbow, fingertip, or knee. Others known as chapel length sweep the floor. Those that extend a few feet onto the floor are called semicathedral length, while veils that match the length of the train are known as cathedral length.

The style of your gown will help you choose the right veil. In addition to considering lengths, you'll want to consider application. How will your hair be done: up, down, half up, half down? Will the veil cover your face, or will it sit high on your head—or even further back? Will you secure it with combs or bobby pins? Will you also wear a headpiece—attached to the veil or separate—or a tiara? These are all things to think about when deciding on your wedding veil. You may know already exactly how you want your veil to be. If not, try on several looks until you find the one you love.

Bride's Accessories

Other accessories that add to your wedding ensemble include shoes, jewelry, stockings, and lingerie. When choosing your bridal shoes, make sure you find a comfortable pair and break them in before the wedding day. Also be sure to wear them to all bridal gown fittings.

For your jewelry, take into consideration your gown's neckline, overall design and formality, the elaborateness of the veil, and the look you're trying to achieve. Sometimes a simple necklace, such as a string of pearls, works best; or to simplify the look even further, you might not wear a necklace at all. Earrings can range from diamond or pearl studs to dangling, drop, or hoop styles.

For your stockings, you'll probably want to get nude-colored or sheer white, and be sure to buy extra pairs in case of a run. Some brides, especially for summer, outdoor, or more casual weddings, or if wearing open-toed shoes, avoid wearing stockings at all. As for your wedding day lingerie, many brides like to wear something frilly and pretty. It's best to wear the bra with wedding gown fittings to make sure straps are hidden and the fit is right.

Making the Bride Beautiful

On the wedding day, Italian brides want to look their absolute best. Many hours prior to the ceremony, the bride is treated to a full beauty session, having her hair and makeup done by professionals. But her physical preparation doesn't begin on the day of the wedding. She often spends several weeks, even months, participating in beauty rituals to get her ready for this day. She is showered with gifts and attention and is given rein to dote on herself, indulging in luxurious bathing and spa treatments, or anything that will help lessen the stress that might otherwise show up in her appearance on the wedding day.

On the morning of the wedding, the Italian bride takes a long, relaxing, aromatic bubble bath. This is not only a cleansing and beautifying experience, but a chance for her to have some quiet time alone before the boisterous festivities begin. Some favored fragrant bath oils include rose and lavender.

Then, the bride has her hair and makeup done, and begins to dress, with the help of her mother and friends.

Pampering Yourself Prior to the Wedding Day

Indulging in beauty rituals prior to and on your wedding day will make you look and feel your best. Your pre-wedding pampering can start as soon as you become engaged, and can be as simple as just making sure you're getting plenty of rest, eating a healthy diet, drinking lots of water, and exercising. You might want to start a fitness program, either at a gym or at home. In addition, you can treat yourself to frequent bathing indulgences at home with fragrant bath oils and bubbles, and perhaps a regular massage, manicure, pedicure, and facial.

You may want to consider scheduling a facial three to four weeks prior to the wedding day. A good facial will improve your skin, clearing away impurities. However, you want to give your skin time to fully expel any blemishes and adjust to changes, which is why you don't want to schedule a facial too close to the wedding day. Other beautifying indulgences include: eyebrow waxing, a manicure, a deep-conditioning treatment for your hair, yoga classes, meditation, surrounding yourself with fresh flowers, or treating yourself to something else you enjoy.

Your Wedding Hair and Makeup

Like the Italian bride-to-be, you'll want to look gorgeous on your wedding day. This often means booking an appointment with a qualified professional hair stylist and makeup artist for the day of your wedding. You can go to them, or they can come to you. Just make sure you book them well in advance, and make sure you have a practice run with both so you know you will like the outcome. Start looking in magazines for hairstyles and makeup that you like and take pictures with you for your practice run. You might even want to emulate the look of an Italian starlet. Also, consider scheduling a nail appointment for a day or two before the wedding.

Attendants' Wardrobe

It is said that the whole notion of bridesmaids and ushers, also called groomsmen, originated in Rome when it was required that ten witnesses be present at a wedding to trick evil spirits who wanted to harm the bride and groom. So that evil spirits would be unable to determine who the bride and groom were, the bridesmaids and ushers all dressed in clothing identical to the bride's and groom's.

Since then, it has remained a tradition that the bridesmaids all dress alike, while the bride is clearly identified. Meanwhile, the groomsmen dress similar to the groom, except for a minor distinguishing mark of some kind, such as a different color tie and boutonniere.

Bridesmaid Dresses

When choosing the dresses your bridesmaids will wear, you will want to keep in mind the style of your wedding gown, your wedding color scheme, wedding logistics, and the bridesmaids' preferences. Shop for them early, preferably right after you select your gown. Depending on the number of bridesmaids you have, shopping for these dresses can be time-consuming between finding a dress that is suitable to all and scheduling fittings. Shoes and accessories will also need to be considered.

Men's Attire

When it comes to what the groom and his attendants will wear on the wedding day, the choices are usually simple. Most often, the men will wear tuxedos or suits. The groom's attire sets the standard for what his groomsmen will wear. Basic tuxedo styles include double-breasted, single-breasted peak, shawl collar, notched collar, and three-button. When choosing the tuxedo style, take into consideration the formality of the wedding. Your wedding gown will play a big role in this, as will the location and time of day and year of your wedding.

Personal Flowers

Since ancient times, brides have carried flowers on their wedding day. Early brides carried bunches of herbs, sometimes consisting of rosemary, garlic, and chives, to symbolize fidelity, fertility, and to ward off evil spirits. It was believed that the odor of these herbs scared off evil spirits and guarded the couple against sickness and bad luck.

Sometimes Roman brides hid these bunches under their veils, which covered their faces, and other times the bride and groom wore floral garlands, which were seen by all. Throughout the years, the tradition of the bride carrying flowers has remained a constant in many cultures. However, the types of flowers chosen have varied. Nowadays, it is rare to see a bride carrying a bunch of strong-smelling herbs, as she is more likely to carry a bouquet of fragrant and elegant blooms.

Italian brides have often worn flowers in their hair, and carried bouquets consisting of orange blossoms, which represented purity and virginity. Even today, the orange blossom is a traditional flower for Italian weddings. This white flower has a sweet delicate scent and a springtime look.

Other favorite flowers for Italian brides include lily of the valley, a symbol of happiness and purity, and roses, which the ancients often used in celebrations, and were believed to bring good luck and protection from evil. Universally, roses are a symbol of love.

Flowers and Their Meanings

Different types of flowers mean different things. Here is a list of flowers and their meanings so you'll know which flowers you'd like to use—and which you should probably avoid.

Amaryllis—splendid beauty

Apple blossom—better things to come; temptation

Bluebells—constancy; humility

Bridal roses—happy love

Buttercup—riches

Camellia—gratitude; admiration; perfection; good luck

Carnation—from an old Italian word meaning complexion; the earliest carnations bore flesh-colored flowers, which gave rise to the name; fascination and love; a sign of a deep and pure love; (pink) "I'll never forget you"; (red) "My heart aches for you"; (yellow) "You have disappointed me."

Chives—believed to promote lust; ward off evil spirits

Chrysanthemum—friendship; cheerfulness; (red) "I love you"; (white) truth

Crocus—cheerfulness

Cyclamen—modesty and shyness

Daffodil—regard

Daisy—innocence; loyalty; purity; daisies symbolize your sharing of feelings; (white) innocence

Dill—believed to promote lust; following the ceremony, it was eaten for that purpose

Fern—fascinations and sincerity

Flowering almond—hope

Forget-me-not—true love and remembrance

Forsythia—anticipation

Gardenia—secret love; joy in a relationship

Garlic—believed to promote lust; ward off evil spirits

Gloxinia—love at first sight

Heliotrope—devotion and faithfulness

Holly—great accent for Christmas time; the ancient Romans used it as a gift of good luck during their winter festivals

Honeysuckle—loveliness; generous and devoted affection

Hyacinth—(blue) constancy; (purple) I'm sorry; (yellow) jealousy

Hydrangea—boastfulness; thank you for understanding

Iris—warmth of affection

Ivy—eternal fidelity; wedded love; everlasting life; friendship; affection; neverending love

Japonica—loveliness

Jasmine—amiability; (yellow) grace and elegance

Lemon blossom—fidelity in love

Lilac—(white) youthful innocence; a first sign of love in a relationship

Lily—majesty; chastity; innocence; purity; virtue; (orange) hatred; (white) purity and modesty

Lily-of-the-valley—return of happiness

Lime—joy in a relationship

Magnolia—preservance; nobility; dignity

Maidenhair—discretion

Mimosa—sensitivity

Myrtle—love; Hebrew emblem of marriage

Nasturtium—patriotism

Orange blossom—purity and virginity; innocence; eternal love; marriage and fruitfulness; the world renowned wedding flower; happiness and fulfillment; lucky when worn by the bride or used in decorations; loveliness

Orchid—love; beauty; refinement; (catalpa) mature charm

Peach Blossom—captive

Peony—happy marriage; a charm against the powers of darkness

Petunia—resentment; anger

Primrose—"I can't live without you"

Rose—symbolizes the brevity of earthly existence; favored bloom for weddings; love; (red) love; desire; (yellow) friendship; also joy and gladness; (coral) desire; (peach) modesty; (dark pink) thankfulness; (deep pink) gratitude; appreciation; (light pink) admiration; sympathy; (pale pink) grace; (orange) fascination; enthusiasm; desire; (white) innocence; also reverence; humility; worthiness; (red and white together) unity; warmth of heart

Rosemary—remembrance; fidelity in love

Snowdrop—hope

Stephanotis—happiness in marriage

Sunflowers—(dwarf) adoration

Sweet pea—delicate pleasures; blissful pleasure

Tulip—love; perfect lover; (red) declaration of love; (yellow) "there's sunshine in your smile"

Veronica—fidelity

Violet—faithfulness; modesty; (blue) faithfulness; (white) "let's take a chance on happiness"

Hyacinths (white) unobtrusive loveliness

Wood sorrel—joy in a relationship

Zinnia—(scarlet) constancy; (white) goodness; (yellow) daily remembrance

Choosing Your Bridal Flowers

An important consideration when assembling your wedding day wardrobe is which flowers will accent the entire look. There are many different thoughts and ideas regarding the bride's and bridesmaids' bouquets. You may decide on certain types of flowers based on their meanings, their scents, or their overall look. You may also consider your overall color scheme, the design and accents of your gown, and the season the wedding takes place.

While orange blossoms, roses, and lilies are favored by most Italian brides for their wedding bouquets, there are still many flower varieties from which to choose. Many arrangements combine several varieties together for a stunning effect. Most bridal bouquets consist of white or mostly white flowers, sometimes with subtle inclusions of pale-colored blooms. Your florist will help you decide on the flowers best suited for your wedding.

Some bouquet styles include: round clustered, also called a nosegay or Colonial style; cascade; hand-tied or loose-tied; traditional or freeform; crescent; clutch; teardrop; heart; oval; arm bouquet or presentation; or a single bloom. And most styles can be arranged in small, medium, and large sizes. You may also consider ordering a separate bouquet to use for the bouquet toss.

For the bridesmaids' flowers, usually a smaller and more colorful variation that complements your own bouquet is chosen. The color of the bridesmaids' dresses, as well as the flowers that are in season when your wedding takes place, will help with your decision.

And don't forget the flowers needed for the corsages for the mothers and grandmothers, as well as boutonnieres for the groom, groomsmen, fathers, and grandfathers, and bouquets or other props for the flower girl, ring bearer, and other special guests.

7

Italian Ceremony Traditions

AT LAST, THE LONG awaited day has arrived, and the bride, groom, family, and friends are about to have the times of their lives.

There are several Italian wedding traditions that take place on the wedding day, before, during and after the ceremony. In this chapter we will explore various Italian wedding customs, of the past and today, and how they can be incorporated into your own wedding.

To Wed or Not to Wed?

In the past, many couples adhered to strict rules and traditions regarding their wedding day. These included who should get married and who should not, and when and when not their wedding should take place.

There would be no wedding if a few crucial factors didn't fall into place. First, according to Italian folklore, uniting in marriage was strongly advised only after all signs pointed to it being favorable. And if the factors did not fall into place, the union was strongly advised against. If there were any indicators of bad luck present in relation to the couple getting married, the marriage surely would be doomed, but if signs of good luck were there, the marriage was sure to be a success.

Everyone involved did all they could to ensure the best possible outcome. And they did it well before the actual wedding day. Most of the time, they believed luck was in their hands—what they did or didn't do would have tremendous effect on whether they had good or bad luck. The bridal couple and their families and friends adhered to the necessary beliefs and customs leading up to the wedding day.

The Right and Wrong Times of the Year

Once it was decided that the couple was a good match and that their marriage would be favorable, another big decision had to be made: when to have the wedding. In Italian tradition, there were definitely right and wrong times of the year to get married. And again, luck was believed to have a lot to do with it.

Marriage was forbidden during Lent and Advent and in the months of May and August. Lent, Advent, and the month of May were to be reserved for holy observations, while getting married in August was just bad luck.

Lent

Lent is the forty-day period that begins on Ash Wednesday and ends on Holy Saturday, the day before Easter. During this time, Christians all over the world prepare for and reflect upon Jesus Christ's death on the cross for the salvation of all, and the Resurrection. For Catholics, Lent is a sacred and spiritual time of prayer and fasting. It reminds them of giving up, of making sacrifices, which in turn reminds them of Christ.

It is believed that by giving up good things, we encourage an attitude of humility, free ourselves from dependence on them, cultivate the spiritual discipline of being willing to make personal sacrifices, and remind ourselves of the importance of spiritual goods over earthly goods. The apostle Paul endorsed the practice of temporary celibacy to engage in a special spiritual discipline of increased prayer. Therefore, a joyous and feasting celebration of marriage was not appropriate during the solemn and reflective time of Lent.

Advent

Advent is another period in the Catholic church that is set aside for prayer and reflection. Although, it doesn't involve the fasting and abstinence associated with Lent, Advent was a time when marriages did not take place. Advent starts on the Sunday nearest to the feast of St. Andrew the Apostle on November 30, and includes the next four Sundays. It can start as early as November 27 and last twenty-eight days, or as late as December 3 and last only twenty-one.

The purpose of Advent is to prepare Catholics for the celebration of Christmas, the birth of Christ, to make their souls worthy of receiving Holy Communion, and therefore make them ready for Christ's final coming at the end of the world. Certain joyous parts of the Mass are not said during Advent, and therefore matrimony (the Nuptial Mass and Benediction) cannot take place. Also, flowers and relics of saints are not to be placed on the altars during this time, except on the third Sunday of Advent.

The Month of May

The next time period that marriage used to be forbidden or warned against was the entire month of May. This was out of respect to Mary, the Mother of God. During this month, Catholics were expected to pay homage to Our Blessed Lady, and they believed that the gifts of God's mercy would come down through Mary in greater abundance during the month of May. All Masses were dedicated to her. As Catholics recognized May as the month to devote completely to Mary, it was therefore improper to hold a marriage ceremony in the Catholic church in May.

The Month of August

And the last period that Italian weddings were not supposed to take place was in the month of August. While the month of August itself was believed to be good luck, getting married in this month was just the opposite. The reason for this is not known exactly, but Italians believed that planning a wedding in August would invite bad luck and sickness.

Good Times to Wed

If these were bad times to get married, cutting into about four months of the year, then what were some favorable times?

A June wedding was considered the luckiest. It was believed that the Roman Goddess Juno watched over, protected, and brought good luck to brides who were married in the month of June. But not everyone could get married in June. Other months that were considered appropriate for getting married were January, February, parts of March and April, July, September, October, and part of November.

And as for days of the week on which to wed, Sunday was the luckiest. A Sunday wedding in the month of June brought the most good fortune to marriages. However, Saturday has always been a suitable day to get married, and today it is the most popular wedding day.

In ancient Italy, it was said that weddings of the higher classes took place early in the morning, often before sunrise, and rarely consisted of celebration. The weddings of the lower classes took place at noon, and featured more festivities.

When selecting the date for your Italian wedding, any month of the year and day of the week that you and your fiancé and your families choose is fine. If you want to keep in complete accordance with Italian tradition, avoid May and August. June has been a favored month by many for numerous reasons, including the superstitious beliefs about it, but also because in most places, the weather in June is almost always the nicest and most reliable. Plus, it's the beginning of summer, flowers are in bloom, and it's a great time to plan a honeymoon vacation. However, when planning a June wedding, make sure you book everything far, far in advance. Because it's a favored month, locations and vendors are often booked two or more years in advance.

Some people choose their wedding date based on meaningful events in their lives, such as their parents' anniversary, an ancestor's birthday, or a favorite holiday or season. Others base it more on practical reasons, like availability of the location, time allotted for planning, or time of the year their out-of-town guests would be most able to travel.

Making the Day Full of Luck

As we've discussed, most people, past and present, want a wedding day that is filled with good fortune. Whether they are superstitious or not, many brides and grooms will participate in such rituals just in case.

And in the Italian culture, you can never do too much to sway fate in the most favorable direction. So, on the wedding day, Italians are often well-prepared to ensure the best possible marriage.

Groom's Good Luck Charm

Long ago, the Italian groom did his part in the pursuit of a blessed marriage by carrying a piece of iron in his pocket on the wedding day. This was believed to ward off the "evil eye" and any supernatural danger that might be drawn to him because of jealousy over his happy situation. Iron was believed to protect the bride and groom from harm and ill-will.

In fact, iron has a long history as a guard against evil. It is believed to be one of the best charms in providing protection against witches, sorcerers, demons, and other evil spirits. In European folklore, iron is said to keep ghosts, mischievous fairies, and other evil spirits away. Ancient Europeans even went so far as to bury iron knives under their doorsteps because witches were scared off by cold iron. In addition, iron has always been a popular metal for creating amulets, which are used to ward off danger and bad luck.

In ancient civilizations, the "evil eye" was a serious threat. It meant different things to different people, and often represented a curse. It could be intentional or not, wicked or harmless. He who received the evil eye often didn't know the intention, but he did what he could to avoid it. If the evil eye represented a curse, it could cause many misfortunes—poverty, loss of love, illness, injury, or death. The evil eye was believed to be provoked by good and happy times, such as a wedding day. That is why it was necessary for the young groom to take precaution.

The actual piece of iron that the Italian groom carried could be any type of object. It may have been an item passed down to the young man by his father, older brother, or relative or friend. Or the groom may have obtained the metal himself. It was usually a very small piece that fit easily into his pocket. Some grooms might reach into their pockets prior to the wedding and cling to the iron piece for extra luck, while others would forget about it as soon they deposited it.

Today, this tradition is easy to incorporate into your wedding. You might consider finding some antique iron piece or coin—at an antique shop, pawnshop, jewelry store, resale store, or online—or consider having one made for the groom especially for this occasion. You might also consider replacing iron with another type of precious metal. Some ideas: gold, silver, platinum, copper, bronze, a brass or iron charm, key ring, money clip, pen, figurine, or trinket of some sort.

The Bride's Good Luck Charm

Italian brides did all they could to invite good luck and discourage ill fate as they prepared for their wedding that day. Many practices involved what the bride wore or avoided wearing.

One such practice involved jewelry. On the day of the wedding, the bride is not supposed to wear any gold until after her ring is slipped on. Wearing gold during or before the wedding was thought to bring bad luck. If you plan to carry out this Italian tradition, you might consider wearing pearls, beads, silver, or platinum jewelry or put your gold jewelry on after the ceremony.

Another item worn by the Italian bride for good luck was the wedding veil. The Italian bride wore a veil because she believed that it would conceal and protect her from evil spirits. Of course, most brides in many cultures wear veils on their wedding days, so this custom is often automatically incorporated into the Italian wedding. However, in the past, Italian brides would often tear their veils, as this was considered good luck. To use this tradition in your Italian wedding, consider carrying an extra piece of tulle for tearing, as you may not want to damage the one you're wearing.

On the Way to the Church

In different parts of Italy, there are various traditions regarding how the bride and groom arrived at the church, who went with whom, and who brought what. Today, these logistics are just as varied. While planning your Italian wedding, you might want to take into consideration the various options.

Bride Arrives Last

In some parts of Italy, it was customary for the bride to arrive at the wedding mass last. In the meantime, the groom would wait in front of the church as his friends, who were supposed to be there to protect him and calm his nerves, teased him trying to make him think the bride might not show up, thus adding to his already nervous state. Of course, this teasing was in good fun, and the groom usually laughed with them knowing that they meant no harm.

The bride, on the other hand, would take her time, purposely delaying her arrival, only adding to the poor groom's nervousness. As the old adage goes, "absence makes the heart grow fonder," and in this case, the bride wanted her future husband to miss her.

The Groom Takes the Bouquet

In Northern Italy, the groom often brought the bouquet of flowers to the wedding. The color and style of the bouquet was supposed to be a surprise to the bride.

This symbolized a gift from the groom's family to the bride. The groom's mother would sometimes help him choose the bouquet.

These days, however, most brides want to select their own bouquets, and along with their florists, coordinate the arrangement in accordance with many other factors, such as the bridal gown, that the groom may not be aware of.

If you wish to incorporate this tradition, you can either let your groom select your bouquet in full faith, or with some guidelines. Or perhaps he could surprise you with a separate smaller bouquet for tossing or keeping. When he presents you with the bouquet that he chose prior to the wedding, make sure you have your photographer capture this romantic moment.

Together to the Church

In the many parts of Italy, the groom walked to the bride's house, and together they and the whole wedding party walked to the church. On the way to the wedding, town residents would watch the group walk by and wish them well. It was a very special opportunity to be able to see a young couple on the way to their wedding.

Sometimes, townspeople would present the bride and groom with little tests of their domestic abilities. For example, they put a broom on the ground and if the bride noticed it and picked it up to put it away she was considered a good housekeeper. A broom is symbolic in many cultures, and has been used in various wedding ceremonies in different ways. For some, the broom is a symbol of "sweeping away what's old to make room for a new life." However, when added to an Italian wedding day, the broom most often represented more domestic traditions. If you plan to use a broom in your wedding ceremony, you might consider purchasing a special ceremonial broom at a craft, cultural, or specialty store, or you might just use a regular house broom that you can decorate to your preference.

If the couple came across a crying child, they were supposed to quiet him and make him smile, and this would mean that they would be good parents. If they came across a beggar and gave him money, it meant that they were giving and good hearted.

Many of the bride's relatives were already at the bride's home when the groom and his family arrived, and together with the groom's family, they would shower the couple with wheat, bread, and salt as the procession continued on to the church.

Some say that wheat, bread, and salt represented abundance, fertility, and good luck. Salt was seen as a symbol of good fortune and in many religions it is believed to keep evil spirits away. It has even been used in exorcisms. Wheat symbolized the symbiosis between a man and a woman, and how each needs the other to grow and prosper. Wheat used for bread represents abundant harvests. The symbolism of wheat was most used in connection with a woman's fertility, and often signified bearing a child and nurturing it, thus transforming nature. Bread and wheat are often used interchangeably; however bread is also used in religion as a sign of life.

You might add some of these Italian wedding day traditions during your adventure to the ceremony. While some brides and grooms don't want to see each other prior to walking down the aisle, others partake in photos and other traditions together long before the ceremony. If the church, or other ceremony site, is within walking distance, it could be a lot of fun to walk there with your bridal party and family. It's a chance to spend some time with your loved ones before the big event, and the physical movement can help calm the nerves. It also gives the photographer an opportunity for additional shots.

Depending on where and how far you will need to walk to your ceremony site, your procession is likely to get lots of attention from "townspeople." However, they most likely won't put you up to any domestic tests. For fun, you could stage your own. Have a pre-party at your home—or your parents' home or wherever you are spending your wedding morning—where friends and family of both the bride and groom meet for breakfast or appetizers and coffee or champagne. Stage the broom test at the party, and have the photographer take a photo. As for the crying child and the beggar tests, you might want to pass. You can have the party shower you with wheat, bread, and salt, but to avoid crumbs in your hair, you might just have them hold up these items while making a toast.

Where the Couple Weds

Just as there were rules for when a couple could be married, there was only one place where the wedding ceremony could take place: a Catholic church. In the old days, anywhere else was not acceptable and the marriage would not be considered real. Although many Italian wedding ceremonies are still held in the Church, today it is acceptable to get married just about anywhere a couple chooses.

A Public Event

In many parts of Italy, even today, when the couple and their procession arrive at the church, there is often a large crowd of onlookers who have come to view the happy couple. Some of these spectators have followed the procession through the town and stopped outside the church to continue their look, while others have arrived before the wedding party knowing that a wedding is to take place there that day. Sometimes the large crowd will stay outside the church during the entire ceremony.

Entering the Church

During many Italian wedding ceremonies, a large bowed ribbon is stretched across the top of the doorways of the church to indicate that someone is "tying the knot" there. The ribbon was used as a symbol of the union of two lives. This is usually how the onlookers found out about the wedding.

These enormous bows are made many different ways and can be many sizes. To make your own, you could buy wide white satin ribbon and tie large bows with long ends draping down. Suspend these bows on as many doorways in the church as you choose, and enhance them with flowers or garnish. Or, go all out and make—or have made—oversized bows out of tulle, satin, cotton, or other material. Using wire and/or starch, shape the material into a giant bow and dangle the ends down to the floor. You might attach wedding bells, flowers, artificial doves, or other wedding symbols and accessories to the middle knot.

Once inside, the entire church was highly ornate. Italy is well known for its beautiful ancient churches, with their elaborate features. Everywhere you looked were breathtaking statues, frescos, stained glass, high ceilings with intricate detail, and beautiful artwork. There were many pews and a long aisle leading to an adorned altar.

On the day of the wedding, the church interior was filled with decorations of all kinds, including floral arrangements, plants, trees, wreaths, garland, ribbon, tapestries, and draped cloths. Flowers—set in vases, pottery, baskets, and on columns—enhanced the foyer, the starting point of the aisle, the sides, the corners, and the areas near the various statues of the saints, Jesus, and the Virgin Mary. Nowadays, it is also common to have a guest book set up in the foyer for guests to sign as they enter the church.

In choosing the flowers and decorations for your wedding ceremony setting, you will want to take into consideration the church or other location and its colors, size, and other details, as well as your bridal flowers, your wedding colors, and the time of year. Choose flowers for the altar, and possibly to place at statues, doorways, corners, at ends of pews, lining the aisle, and wherever else you deem appropriate. We will discuss this more in chapter 11, when talking about setting the stage.

The Ceremony Begins

As guests begin to arrive, music often starts to play. This can be recorded music, an organ, band, choir, singer, harp, trio, or whatever you like, as we will discuss more in chapter 10. Guests are often escorted to their seats by ushers or groomsmen, the bride's family to the left and the groom's to the right. Meanwhile, the groom and best man wait in a private room, and the bride and bridesmaids in another. After the guests are seated, the groom's mother is seated, followed by the bride's mother. Once the bride's mother is seated, the ceremony officially begins. Sometimes the ushers will roll out a white aisle runner. It was believed by many cultures that this symbolized "walking on holy ground."

The priest, groom, and best man approach the altar and wait. Groomsmen enter from the side and meet up with bridesmaids who are walking in from the back of the church, and finish their walk to the altar together. The ring bearer and flower girls then enter, followed by the maid of honor. Processional music begins and the bride, usually accompanied by her father on her left, walks down the aisle, as the congregation stands. The bride's father hands her off to the groom and they turn and face the altar together. In most ceremonies, the bride stands at the left, and the groom on the right, as it was believed by the ancient Romans that the groom should keep his right arm free to grab his sword if danger approached.

The Wedding Mass

In the Catholic Church, the wedding celebration is one of the seven sacraments. The sacraments, which also include Baptism, Eucharist, Confession, Confirmation, Holy Orders, and Annointing of the Sick, are known as channels to God's grace.

While couples have been engaging in marriage rituals from the beginning of time, the notion of the religious wedding ceremony evolved through the years and became a second part of the original marriage ritual.

In the Renaissance era, the concept of marriage was different. In the eyes of the Church, the only requirement for a valid marriage was the exchange of vows between a consenting couple and the consummation of their union. Often, the couple might attend mass after their marriage.

However, many of the wedding rituals that now take place during church ceremonies originated outside of the church, sometimes literally right outside the church door. These included parental discussion, dowry exchanges, and the exchange of rings, all of which were crucial to the public nature of the ceremony.

Long ago, in many parts of Italy, it was common for the marriage contract to be made in the presence of a priest, who would lead Mass upon completion. The announcement of the union was made pubic shortly thereafter.

From the beginning, marriage has been considered a contract between two people, and therefore worthy of blessing. The church recognized marriage as a holy endeavor, and now wedding ceremonies are held in churches of every denomination.

The church first became involved in the marriage ritual by urging the couple to attend the special nuptial mass. This mass represents a high form of blessing to a marriage, and is very much today like the one that started with the Romans centuries ago.

In fact, the Catholic marriage ceremony, much like its early days, is said to have two parts. The preliminaries, also know as the betrothal or "sponsalia," are the expressed consent of the couple to be married and their parents' approval. The second part is the actual execution of the pledges, also known as "subarrhatio." This is represented by the exchanging of the rings, the handing over of the dowry in front of witnesses, the celebration of Mass, and the solemn benediction. In ancient times, the benediction included the priest holding a veil over the married couple and the pair wearing crowns as they left the church.

Today, the Catholic wedding ceremony consists of a declaration of consent made by a man and a woman, the blessing of the rings, short versicles, and a benedictory prayer, followed by the nuptial mass.

The Catholic Wedding Ceremony

The Catholic wedding ceremony is full of spirituality and meaningful symbolism. It generally follows the sequence below.

An Offertory The bride places flowers on the shrine of the Blessed Virgin Mary as musicians play "Ave Maria."

Introductory Rites An opening prayer in which the priest greets the couple and asks for God's blessing on their wedding day.

Liturgy of the Word Biblical reading by the priest and a friend or family member, followed by the priest's sermon about marriage.

Rite of Marriage The congregation stands as the couple make their vows, declaring their commitment to one another.

Exchange of Rings After the couple says "I do," the best man gives the bride's ring to the priest, who blesses it and hands it to the groom to place on her finger. Then, the maid of honor gives the groom's ring to the priest, who blesses it and hands it to the bride to place on the groom's finger. The bride and groom each say "I take this ring as a sign of my love and faithfulness in the name of the Father, the Son, and the Holy Spirit."

Nuptial Mass The priest leads the sign of peace, and the congregation shakes hands, and Holy Communion follows. Finally, the priest says a closing prayer and nuptial blessing asking for strength and protection for the couple. He presents the new couple, and says, "You may kiss the bride." He finishes with "Mass has ended, you may go in peace."

Some Important Aspects

During the Catholic wedding ceremony, there are various important customs that take place. Many of these elements are seen in non-Catholic weddings as well. And some can be personalized to fit your own preferences.

Giving the Bride Away

The father of the bride walks his daughter down the aisle and gives her away. This tradition evolved from the time when the bride's father was giving up his position as the bride's caretaker, and was blessing the groom to take over. Today, this tradition is practiced by many cultures and is a sentimental part of the wedding ceremony.

Special Readings

During your wedding ceremony, you may choose a family member, friend, or bridal party member to present a reading of your choice. Again, the priest may assist in choosing readings or you or the reader may make the choice. Sometimes readings are Biblical passages, parables, or appropriate selections from other books, or poems or other pieces written by you or a loved one.

Wedding Vows

When it comes to your wedding vows, you have many choices. There are many standard vows that have stood the test of time and are as meaningful today as they were many years ago. Some vows fit some couples better than others.

When planning your wedding, make sure to talk to your priest about options regarding your wedding vows. He may have a set of vows, or several sets that he prefers to use. He may be open to you finding vows you like, writing your own, or helping you choose. You might even consider saying some of your vows in Italian.

Wedding Rings

The exchanging of wedding rings is a very important part of the marriage ceremony. Almost all cultures incorporate this ancient tradition into the celebration. The giving of rings represented a pledge between the bride and groom, their promise to be faithful. The wedding ring symbolizes neverending love because of its circular shape. The wedding ring is placed on the fourth finger of the left hand, because it was believed that the vein in that finger ran directly to the heart.

According to Roman tradition, wedding rings, continuous circles with no beginning and no end, symbolized eternal love. The ancient Romans used precious stones as well as silver and gold in the rings, which were carried on a cushion. The ring bearer or maid of honor would carry the cushion up the aisle to the best man, who would place the rings on the altar to be blessed.

Eucharistic Benediction

Catholic wedding masses include the Eucharistic Benediction, which represents the devotion to the Eucharist Christ. It consists of the showing, blessing, praising,

The Italian countryside—
what could be a more
romantic location for a
wedding?

A typical Naples family

A few Italian ancestors: my great-grandfather,
grandfather, great-aunt, and great-uncle

Great-uncle Tony and great-aunt Doris on their wedding day

My great-aunt Ida as a bride

My contemporary Italian family, from left: Uncle Sammy, Uncle George, Grandpa Tony, Aunt Doris, and Aunt Dana

Steve and Sophia
and their
wedding party

An alternative to
the traditional
Italian wedding:
My mom and dad
after they tied the
knot in Las Vegas
in 1966

Steve and Sophia Canfora Antal
on their wedding day,
October 18, 1941

The Granieri wedding bridesmaids in matching powder-pink gowns

The Wyants get married in a typical church wedding in Italy

A panorama of Florence

and offering of the Blessed Sacrament, or Holy Communion, often accompanied by hymns. The priest makes the sign of the cross with the sacrament and recites the Divine Praises.

Kissing the Bride

In ancient Rome, the kiss exchanged by a bride and groom on their wedding day represented a legal bond that sealed their marriage contract.

After the Ceremony

Once the wedding ceremony is complete, the fun begins. The serious part is replaced with festive frivolity almost instantly. Right after the priest announces the couple, they share a kiss and he announces that Mass is over. Then the joyful couple pause for a moment as their guests applaud and upbeat music plays.

The Recessional

After the ceremony, the bride and groom lead the recession down the aisle. They are followed by the flower girl and ring bearer, then the maid of honor and best man, bridesmaids and groomsmen, parents, and the rest of the congregation.

The bride and groom are sometimes swept into a room in the back of the church, often with their bridal party, as the guests file out to the front of the church. During this brief interlude the couple may have a chance to be alone and reflect on the significant event that just took place. This is also an opportunity for members of the bridal party to congratulate them.

Confetti

Once the guests are assembled outside in front of the church, the bride and groom, followed by the bridal party, make their way through the crowd and off to the next location. In the past, the Italian newlywed couple was showered with rice or paper confetti as they came out of the church after the ceremony. Confetti and rice represented wishes for abundance in money and good fortune in their new life together. Sometimes flower petals and herbs were thrown to further protect the couple from evil spirits. And sometimes, in Northern Italy, the couple was showered with cakes, bread, and baked goods. In some places money was thrown at the couple.

Even today, confetti comes showering onto the couple by all the surrounding well wishers as they exit the church. However, it is no longer acceptable to throw uncooked rice, as it is harmful to birds. Confetti consists of little pieces of colored paper and streamers. You can find it at craft stores or you can make your own. Scraps from hole punches and paper shredders make great confetti. You can save it up over time, or you can buy colored paper and punch away. Then, gather the tiny pieces into stacks—about the size of a handful or two—and put them into little sacks made of paper, tulle, or another type of material, or into hollowed out, clean, dry eggshells and make them available to guests to toss. Other alternatives to confetti can be birdseed, flower petals, or bubbles.

Doves

At some Italian weddings, a pair of white doves is released to symbolize the couple's love and happiness. The dove is a symbol of peace and purity and is used to represent the soul and the Holy Spirit. In addition, because doves are often lifelong partners with their companions, they also represent affection and commitment.

You might include doves in your wedding ceremony by having them released once you exit the church. There are several companies now that provide doves for such releases. Check your local phone book or the Internet.

Back Through Town

In the small towns and villages of Italy, after the ceremony the newlyweds would walk through town, greeting their friends, families, and neighbors. Sometimes townspeople would set up a sawhorse, a log, and a double-handled rip saw. According to tradition, the couple must saw the log in two. This represents the working together of the couple throughout their lifetime.

For your Italian wedding, you might incorporate the walk through town if your reception location is near the ceremony. You and your guests could walk there together. And you might include the sawhorse tradition in your wedding day on a smaller scale, perhaps right outside the church, or along your walk.

Nowadays, it is common for the bridal party to stay behind at the church, or relocate somewhere to take wedding pictures while their guests go to the reception site ahead of them. After pictures, the bridal party is often driven to the reception site.

8

Italian Reception Traditions

AFTER THE ELABORATE CEREMONY, the Italian wedding festivities begin. It's time for a true Italian traditional event with an abundance of food, music, dancing, and more customs. What is it about an Italian wedding reception that makes it like no other? Everything! In fact, it is the reception itself that makes an Italian wedding an Italian wedding!

Ask anyone about Italian weddings, they'll likely mention the activities that take place after the ceremony—the fun they had, drinking too much wine, indulging themselves in an endless assortment of food, and dancing until dawn. They might even mention some of the traditional rituals practiced by the bride, groom, attendants, and guests.

Food is a huge part of the Italian wedding reception, and we will discuss it further in chapter 9. And there are many traditions related to music and dancing, which will be explored in chapter 10. Right now, we will look at some of the other aspects of the traditional Italian wedding reception.

The Atmosphere of the Italian Wedding Reception

The Italian wedding reception has an energy that is immediately apparent. The feeling is spirited, upbeat, and festive right from the start. The mood is positive and joyful, as all guests know they are there to celebrate one of life's most treasured events. In the Italian culture, a wedding is a major event and is anticipated for a long time in advance. In fact, in the old days, relatives and family friends of the bride have looked forward to this day since she was a little girl. It's a sentimental time, and everyone is happy to be there.

Where the Reception Is Held

Long ago, Italian wedding receptions mainly took place at the bride's former home. Oftentimes, after the procession left the church and walked back through town, they would end up in front of the bride's parents' home. There the immediate family would go inside for an intimate dinner and the rest of the town would enjoy drinks and appetizers outside. Then, everyone would reconvene for more drinks, music, and dancing.

Weddings in some parts of Italy would carry on for two weeks. During this time the bride would not go out of the house. She would stay in and receive gifts and money from the many visitors who would stop by to shower congratulations. Other couples would leave on their honeymoon right away, returning to receive these gifts during the following weeks. Often, while they were gone, the families of the bride and groom would carry on the celebration with dinner parties and get-togethers in their honor.

In more recent times, many wedding receptions in Southern Italy have been taking place at restaurants and hotel banquet rooms, often overlooking the ocean. These elegant settings, with their breathtaking views, have become popular choices for those who can afford them. Meanwhile, in the smaller villages, celebrations continued at the bride's or groom's parents' home—whichever was larger.

Nowadays, receptions can be held just about anywhere, as long as there is plenty of room for the hundreds of guests. Brides and grooms everywhere are planning their celebrations at the standard locations, such as a home or banquet hall, and more creative sites, like a vineyard or a museum.

When choosing the location for your Italian wedding reception, you will want to consider a venue that will easily accommodate the number of guests to be invited and the activities planned. Some important considerations will be: having enough space for dance floor, band or DJ, plenty of tables and serving areas; whether the location is close to the ceremony site; price; availability; formality and style; and whether the space lends itself to the atmosphere you are trying to create, which we will discuss more in chapter 11.

The People at the Reception

As already mentioned, family is of the utmost importance in the Italian culture, and when it comes to Italian wedding celebrations, this cannot be overlooked. The family and close friends the bride and groom invite to celebrate with them on their day is a big part of the reception tradition. Part of what makes this occasion so special and sentimental is sharing it with the right people.

At any Italian wedding reception, just look around the room and you'll see people hugging, kissing, shaking hands, slapping each other on the back, reminiscing, sharing stories, laughing, crying, and enjoying each other's company. You'll see priests breaking bread with bankers and businessmen, and young children on the dance floor with great-grandmothers. It is a very social event in which everyone is family.

How the Reception Begins

Once guests have left the church, they make their way to the reception site, which is already decorated and usually set up with a bar and tables with appetizers.

Background music plays, and servers make their way around the room, offering champagne and hors d'oeuvres from trays. Guests start mingling and indulging long before the bride and groom arrive.

The Best Man's Role

In Italian weddings of old, the best man greeted guests as they came into the reception. Upon welcoming them, he would offer them a drink from a tray of liquor. Traditionally sweet liquors, such as crème de cacao or Galliano, were served to the women and strong drinks, like whisky or gin, were offered to the men.

The drinks were served to kick off the festivities and to give everyone the opportunity to make toasts in the newlyweds' honor before they arrived. The best man would often move around the room to lead toasts to the bride and groom with various groups of guests.

In the old days, the best man was an integral part of the wedding celebration, and had to be a responsible and established individual. Sometimes he was a relative or the godfather of the bride, or a long-time family friend of the bride and groom. It was often his responsibility to help out financially with the wedding and other future needs of the newlyweds.

Long ago in Venice, the best man was expected to pay for all the wine and liquor for the wedding reception. In addition, he was in charge of giving money to the children and the beggars in the street as they made their way from the church to the reception site. He would also make all arrangements for gondolas to take the guests to the reception site.

In more recent times, the best man has become less involved in the wedding, serving mainly as a supporter to the groom. He is often a brother, cousin, or good friend of the groom, and his responsibilities mainly include leading a toast to the couple before supper. However, you can follow Italian tradition more closely and make your best man a more vital part of the wedding celebration.

The groom might start by choosing someone who he feels would be willing and honored to actively participate in various wedding activities, such as greeting guests upon arrival, acting as an emcee or host for the day, going from table to table welcoming guests and asking if they need anything, and making a speech on the couple's behalf, in which he welcomes guests and honors and thanks the parents and others involved in giving the wedding. Or, you might assign the best man and the maid of honor to take on these extra duties, or appoint another relative or friend to greet guests as they arrive.

It's in the Bag

A well-known and much-practiced Italian wedding tradition involves a little white satin purse carried by the bride. Known as "la borsa," "buste," or "passing the hat," this custom allows the bride and groom to acquire some money on their wedding day. Guests take turns placing envelopes filled with cash in the bag. In Italy throughout the years, it has been common for elders to give money to younger relatives. And it was considered polite to conceal the amount of money in an envelope. It hardly seemed materialistic for the bride to carry the "buste" specifically for this purpose.

From the moment guests arrived, they would approach the bride and groom, congratulate them with hugs and slip them the envelope. This would go on throughout the evening. When the purse was not in the bride's possession, her mother or grandmother would guard it for her. And at the end of the night, the bride and groom would count up the money they received, often surprised by the generosity of the guests. Sometimes this money would be used to pay for their honeymoon.

At some receptions, all the men would dance with the bride, having to deposit money in the purse in order to do so. This is done at many weddings for different cultures today, and is often referred to as "the money dance." An Italian woman I know says the money dance is not practiced at traditional Italian weddings, and she would not permit it at her daughters' weddings.

If you plan to follow the Italian buste tradition, you might be concerned about how to go about it. How do you inform your guests that they should bring money envelopes to place in your purse?

One way is to let them know ahead of time about the various Italian wedding traditions that will take place at your wedding. You can do this through a wedding newsletter, in which you communicate to your guests tidbits about the two of you, your backgrounds, your upcoming wedding, and anything else you'd like to share. It's a great way to let your guests get to know you both and be even more a part of your special day. You might mention what the buste tradition is, along with other traditions and what they mean to you.

Or you can let guests know ahead of time by word of mouth. Mention it to close family members and friends who might tell others. Or talk about it at your bridal shower, engagement party, or at some other event. Another alternative is on the day of the wedding have the DJ, band leader, or emcee make an announcement regarding the buste tradition, telling guests they can pick up envelopes at a certain spot. You can also set up a basket at the guest book or other table filled with envelopes and a written explanation of the custom. Guests can pick up an envelope and participate in the tradition if they choose. Add an extra element by having little pieces of paper and pencils, on which guests can write a note of congratulations, advice, or other sentiment to include in the envelope—either with the money or in its place.

As for the purse itself, you can use any number of white satin bridal purses available at bridal shops or through catalogs. Or you may choose to make your own buste. Choose a thick satiny material, or for a layered approach, a solid material for underneath and a sheer patterned material on top. You can make your own pattern from paper in a shape you like—rectangular, round, or pear-shaped. Cut it out and trace it onto the material, then cut the material. Sew up the seams, leaving an opening at the top. For straps, string pearl-like beads on wire or thick reed.

Breaking Glass

At Italian weddings, specifically in Southern Italy, it was traditional for the bride and groom to break a glass or a vase and then count up the number of pieces that remained. The pieces represented the number of happy years of marriage the couple could expect. While the practice of breaking glass takes place in other cultures, the symbolism behind it varies. In an Italian wedding, this practice usually would take place near the end of the celebration as it signified what was next for the couple. The couple usually aimed to smash the glass as hard as they could, thus guaranteeing the largest amount of pieces. They also tried to find a type of glass that shattered easily. Then someone would help them count up the pieces of broken glass—hopefully without getting cut. The number would sometimes be in the hundreds, which of course was a very good sign.

If you plan to partake in breaking glass at your wedding, there are some precautions you must take. Breaking glass is sometimes messy and can be dangerous, especially if children are present. Make sure the breaking is done in a spot where it won't scatter too far, and that someone is there to clean it up completely. And when you or someone else is counting up the broken pieces, make sure to have some garden or rubber gloves available, and have the area swept afterward. You may want to keep your broken glass pieces in a jar as a reminder of your many years of happiness.

Cutting the Necktie

Another Italian wedding tradition that took place at the traditional Italian wedding reception was "the cutting of the tie." The best man cut the groom's tie into little pieces, put the pieces on a tray, and sold them to the guests. The money received was used to help pay for the band or the honeymoon. This was a fun, lighthearted activity that everyone enjoyed.

To add this tradition to your wedding, consider getting an extra tie for cutting. The best man can cut it into pieces in front of guests or the tie can be cut up ahead of time. Two or three ties might even be used. Or you can leave the tray of tie pieces on a table with a box for guests to deposit their payment for a piece.

Toasting the Newlyweds

It is a tradition at most weddings to toast the wedding couple. Most often, the best man proposes a toast prior to dinner, and sometimes the maid of honor, fathers of the bride and groom, and various other individuals toast as well.

It has always been common at Italian weddings for the newlyweds to receive several toasts throughout the entire event. It would often start with the best man, sometimes prior to the couple's arrival and again just before dinner.

During the reception, various wedding attendees would make toasts to the newlywed couple as well. A common toast would be "Per cent'anni," which means "for a hundred years." Another is "Evviva la sposa!" or "long live the bride!" And "Evviva gli sposi!" or "hurray for the newlyweds!"

Love Is in the Air

At some Italian wedding receptions, a pair of white doves is released into the air, symbolizing the couple's love and happiness. If the releasing of the doves doesn't take place during or immediately following the ceremony, it sometimes takes place at the reception. At an outdoor event, the releasing of doves is relatively easy to do. Otherwise, the birds can be released out of a window, off a balcony, or outside the reception site.

You might set aside a certain time during the reception to release the doves. A speech or poem could be included prior to or during the release in connection with a toast, in honor of a loved one who has passed away, or as the conclusion of the celebration.

An alternative to releasing doves is to include them in an ornate cage as part of the décor and ambience. See chapter 12 for more details.

Tricks and Pranks

During the Italian wedding reception, it has been customary for the bridal party and other friends of the bride and groom to tease and pull pranks on the newlyweds. For example, the groomsmen and other male friends might kiss the bride to make the groom jealous, as well as to bring the couple good luck. Sometimes they'd take turns dancing with the bride, so much that the groom hardly had a chance to dance with her.

Friends of the groom would also sneak away to play tricks on the new couple. Also known as "tricking the place," most of these pranks involved the newlyweds' home. Some included putting itching powder in their bed, nailing their front door closed which made it difficult for them to enter, and then later showing up at their house at all hours of the night begging for food.

Some of these pranks are a little extreme, and you probably won't want to include them in your wedding. However, there are more civilized ways to have some fun with tricks. The friends of the bride and groom might want to surprise them with some silly props found in magic shops—the spilled milk, can of worms, oversized ball and chain—or with little notes scattered around. They could embarrass the newlyweds with a silly singing telegram to show up at some later time. Or, for another twist, the friends might surprise the couple with something thoughtful—cleaning their house, buying them groceries, a basket of fruit, flower arrangements, or a big banner saying "congratulations," and a bunch of balloons.

Jordan Almonds

Traditionally called "confetti" or "bombonièra," an assortment of Jordan almonds wrapped in tulle and tied with ribbon is often featured at Italian weddings. While this tradition has to do with food, it is considered to be separate from the "feast" foods to be covered later. The custom of Jordan almonds has less to do with eating and more to do with symbolism. And these almonds make great wedding favors.

Long ago, mesh bags filled with Jordan almonds were tossed at the bride and groom—like confetti—as a symbol of fertility. Although the actual tossing of these bags of hard candy is rarely practiced anymore, they are still included at many Italian weddings. In addition to being a symbol of fertility, Jordan almonds represent the "union of bitter and sweet" or the give-and-take of married life. While the fresh almonds have a bittersweet taste, much like life, the sugar coating represents the wish for more sweetness for the newlyweds in life than bitterness.

The number of Jordan almonds in a cluster is usually five, representing health, wealth, happiness, fertility, and long life. Also having an odd number is a symbol of the connected and "indivisible" nature of marriage.

In the past, instead of wedding cake, ornamental bags or boxes were filled with the sugared almonds and sent to friends and guests. Sometimes the bags of Jordan almonds are placed on a silver tray, which the bride and groom carry around and offer to guests. The bride will also use a spoon to hand them to the guests.

The sugar-coated almonds come in a variety of colors, and can be purchased at Italian markets, gourmet food shops, wedding shops, and various specialty stores. They come in packages of single or assorted colors—usually pastel pink, green, blue, yellow, and white.

To make your own "confettò" or "bombonièra" estimate the number of guests, multiply that by five, and purchase enough Jordan almonds to have a little extra. Buy tulle at a fabric store—you can also order pre-cut tulle circles from wedding specialty catalogs and shops. If you are buying fabric, measure the size of material you will need for each favor. A good rule of thumb for five Jordan almonds is a 9-inch circle—the size of a paper plate. You may choose smaller or larger. Practice first with a paper tower, using a plate or other round object as a pattern.

Once you've purchased the tulle, cut out the circles, place the five—or amount of your choice—Jordan almonds in the center, and tie with ribbon. You can buy ribbon—whatever material and size your prefer—at a fabric store, or you can order it personalized with your first names and your wedding date from a wedding specialty catalog. You can also attach a small card to the bundles explaining the significance and traditional background of these treats.

Instead of wrapping Jordan almonds in tulle, you can place them in readymade bags, pretty boxes, or some other container. Also, the Jordan almonds can be replaced with some other kind of candies or mints.

Bride and Groom Make Rounds

As mentioned, the bride and groom may choose to travel from table to table handing out the Jordan almond bunches from a silver tray. This gives them a chance to greet each guest individually. It is also customary for the bride and groom to make their rounds without the tray of treats, specifically to thank everyone for coming and allowing the guests to congratulate them. They might do this after dinner and before dancing and dessert. This can be instead of or in addition to a receiving line.

Cutting the Cake

It is traditional for the Italian bride and groom to partake in the popular custom of cutting the wedding cake. This takes place sometime during the reception after dinner and some dancing. The groom will place his right hand over the bride's right hand and her left hand is placed on top. The bride then positions the knife at the center of the bottom tier of the cake and slowly cuts the cake with the groom. They then share the first slice together. More about Italian wedding cakes will be discussed in chapter 9.

The Bouquet and Garter

At many Italian weddings today, the bride and groom participate in the bouquet and garter customs. The bride will toss her bouquet—or another bouquet made especially for tossing—to a group of single women. The belief has always been that the one who catches the bouquet is the next to be married.

During the garter toss, the bride sits in a chair as the groom takes the garter from her leg and tosses it out to the single men. The man and woman who catch these objects are usually photographed together with the bride and groom.

Bride and Groom Sneak Away

It was customary at Italian weddings of the past for the newlywed couple to quietly and inconspicuously sneak away while the reception was still going on. Sometimes they would leave for their honeymoon right away, and other times they'd retire to their home, where they might find the tricks their friends had played. Even after the bride and groom left, the reception would continue until late into the night.

Other Italian brides and grooms made a grand exit at the end of the night. Sometimes they would even change into departure clothes and then say goodbye to everyone there. As they left, the guests would follow them out and watch them drive or be driven away.

These days, brides and grooms leave the reception in many different ways. Some might quietly duck out, saying goodbye only to their parents and a close few others. Some make their exit known, saying goodbye to guests individually or making an announcement to all. At some weddings, the band leader or DJ might announce and play a last song of the evening, after which the guests follow the newlyweds out the door.

For your wedding, you'll want to decide what kind of exit suits you best. You might consider changing into a special departure outfit, or you may want to surprise your guests with a special last dance, an announcement, or presentation of a gift to your parents or new husband.

The Getaway Car

Once the newlyweds left, either quietly or announced, they would hop into their getaway car, which in ancient times may have been a horse and carriage—or in Venice, a gondola—and more recently, an automobile.

The bridal party would decorate the front of the bridal car with flowers, symbolizing happy travels throughout life together.

As the newlyweds made their way through the streets, the locals would come out and cheer and wish them well, as they tossed bread, cakes, and other baked goods at them, again symbolizing good luck, fertility, and a prosperous future.

Many couples these days leave their weddings in a limousine, which takes them home or to their honeymoon—or to the airport to go on their honeymoon. Some couples drive away in their own cars, and still others come up with imaginative alternatives.

For your getaway car, you might consider renting an Italian car, such as a Ferrari, Fiat, or Lamborghini. Or for fun, and if you don't have far to go, ride off together on a Vespa. If you're near water, you could hire someone to take you off in a gondola. Or you can charter a horse and carriage.

Whatever you choose for your getaway car, decorate it with a garland of flowers on the front grill. Secure garland along the sides and a sign on the back that says "Evviva gli sposi!" or "hurray for the newlyweds."

Entering the Home

Before the newlyweds arrived together at their new home, some well-wishers had been there to leave their mark, in addition to "tricking the place."

Sometimes, especially in Southern Italy, the bride's and groom's mothers would go to the home a few days before the wedding and "make the bed." The mothers put money under their own child's pillow, and together they would decorate the entire bed with confetti and money pinned to the sheets. This was believed to bring the couple wealth and good fortune. Some relatives would sew the bed sheets together to make the wedding night tricky for the newlyweds.

When the Italian bride and groom arrived at their new home, they would often find that a ribbon had been tied to the front door. This symbolized the union of two lives and served as a sign of good luck.

Upon entering the home, the groom would usually carry the bride over the threshold. This is a custom that has been practiced many years by various cultures, and is said to symbolize different things. Some say this tradition stemmed from the days when a man would steal a bride and carry her home against her will. In early Rome, the groom would drag the bride into the home because she wanted to stay with her parents. Others say it is based more on superstition than barbaric practices. It was believed that evil spirits lurked at the doorway, so the groom had to carry the bride into the home to protect her. Another belief from Roman days was that it was bad luck for the bride to trip over the doorway upon her first arrival in her new home. So to avoid any problems, the groom just picked her up and carried her in. Nowadays, it just seems like more of a romantic notion than anything else.

Other Reception Activities to Consider

Aside from Italian wedding traditions involving food, drink, music, and dance, which will be covered later in separate chapters, there are several other reception activities to consider, such as having a cocktail/social hour before the meal, or perhaps at a different location than your reception site. This might be a patio outside the church, a restaurant on the way to the reception site, someone's home, or in another banquet room where your reception is being held.

A receiving line at the reception, as you and the bridal party arrive, is an option, giving you a chance to say hello to all of your guests before the festivities begin. You can do this during the cocktail hour so you and guests can mingle while sipping a beverage and having a snack.

A grand entrance and introduction of the bride, groom, and bridal party is a great way to begin the festivities. The band leader, DJ, or an emcee or close friend can do the introductions, while the music of your choice plays in the background.

You might consider having a prayer or blessing said before the meal. This can be led by the priest who married you, the best man, or any other special friend or relative.

Italian Wedding Food

FOOD! THE CENTRAL THEME of the Italian wedding, and all Italian celebrations for that matter, is the succulent fare of the country admired for its culinary quintessence. And what's even better than the food itself is the abundance of it! An Italian wedding without food is like an Italian wedding without wine, music, family, friends, and laughter—it just doesn't happen.

Italian weddings through the years have always emphasized food. In ancient Rome, a loaf of wheat bread was broken over the heads of the bride and groom to ensure a fertile and fulfilling life. Guests would eat the crumbs for good luck. Since then, the notion of breaking bread has stuck, only the variety has changed. Now the wedding feast consists of up to fourteen courses, sometimes more.

In addition to the multicourse dinner, Italian weddings often feature symbolic foods like bowties, or "wanda," which are twists of fired dough, powdered with sugar (see chapter 14 for recipe), Italian wedding candy, wedding cake, and a variety of pastries. Dinner is accompanied by wine and dessert is served with espresso, coffee, and sweet liqueurs.

In this chapter, we will look at the some typical Italian wedding courses and provide examples and suggestions for each course, from appetizer to main dish to dessert. We will explore the special cuisine of each of Italy's regions, as well as what is involved in hiring a caterer and selecting a wedding cake. Then, we will examine the beverages—wines, champagne, coffees, and liqueurs.

Italians and Their Food

The food of Italy is an experience in and of itself with all of its rich colors, shapes, textures, aromas, and flavors. In fact, one of the main reasons people visit Italy is for the food. World-renowned restaurants and trattorìa serve up a little bit of heaven that keeps people coming back time after time.

The food of Italy stirs up an array of sensory awareness, engaging not only the taste buds and sense of smell, but sight and feeling as well. The colors are vibrant—red sauces, yellow pastas, green peppers, purple onions, and deep magenta wines. The shapes are varied—triangular frittata slices, square lasagna pieces, round calamari rings, and funnel-shaped cannoli. The textures and temperatures complement each other, with cool meats, piping hot melted cheese, temperate wines, steamed cappuccino, and iced gelato. From dry focaccia to mouth-watering veal cutlets, the flavors run the gamut with the sweet, spicy, mild and subtle, rich and full-bodied, salty, zesty, creamy, and refreshing.

Even from the early days, food has been an important part of the Italian way of life, specifically in celebrations. Early banquets were plentiful, as witnessed by the sumptuous feasts of the Romans. Somewhere along the way food became equated with happiness and the good life. Social beings participated in a good share of tournaments and celebrations of various types, all of which emphasized the feast. And these feasts kept getting bigger and bigger, with more and more courses, until they turned into what they are today.

The huge celebratory meal with its many servings and enormous portions has become a representation of Italy in America. It has become synonymous with happy occasions, and Italians know they will find it at most celebrations.

The Food that Feasts Are Made Of

With Italians, food is a gala that is celebrated with gusto. The Italian meal is a slow dance, every bite savored. Traditional meals can last for hours.

The traditional Italian meal usually starts with an antipasto, followed by pasta or risotto, sometimes soup, meat and/or fish, cheese, vegetables or salad, and then dessert with coffee. The following are some examples of what might be featured in each course. These can vary from region to region, which we'll look at later:

Antipasto Cold cuts of meat and seafood, calamari, shrimp, salami, prosciutto, cheeses like mozzarella and provolone, mortadella, cold vegetable dishes, peppers, pepperoncini, pickles, olives, marinated mushrooms, stuffed mushrooms, marinated artichoke hearts, pimentos, sliced tomatoes, melon, prosciutto wrapped around provolone sticks.

Appetizers (included within, in addition to, or instead of antipasto) Roasted garlic served with French bread, Italian mushrooms stuffed with peppers and breadcrumbs, marinated mushrooms and cheese, carpaccio (raw beef), peppers and anchovies, marinated mozzarella, fried calamari, pizza rustica (meat-filled pastry), quiche, fried mozzarella, canapés (round bread with anchovy paste and sliced olives), Mediterranean frittata, spinach gnocchi, shrimp cocktail, marinated fresh anchovies (with olive oil, garlic, and lemon juice), fried eggplant, eggplant Parmesan, deep pan pizza cut into squares, roasted asparagus with prosciutto.

Breads Garlic bread, Parmesan toast, dinner rolls, focaccia (made with pizza dough), bruschetta (with olive oil, garlic, and chopped tomatoes), bread sticks, cheese bread (with mozzarella cheese melted on it), pizza, calzone, polenta (made from fried cornmeal).

Salads Mixed green salad, green salad with tomatoes, Caesar salad, antipasto salad (lettuce with meats, cheeses, and olives), pasta salad, tomato, mozzarella and basil salad, eggplant salad, Panzanella (Italian bread salad), salade Niçoise (tuna, tomatoes, anchovies, greens, and hardboiled egg), fennel, olive and radicchio salad, marinated vegetable salad.

Soups Roasted garlic soup, pasta fagiole, minestrone, pasta and bean soup, gazpacho (cold vegetable soup with vinegar), meatball soup, cioppino (fish soup).

Pasta Dishes Spaghetti alla Bolognese (with ground beef and tomato sauce); fettuccine alla carbonara (bacon and cheese sauce); ravioli (stuffed with spinach, cheese, or meat); lasagna, fettuccine Alfredo (white Parmesan cheese sauce); spaghetti al tartufo (truffle); angelhair pasta with tomato; classic pesto with linguine (basil leaves and pine nuts); risotto alla Milanese (short grain rice with saffron); pasta primavera (fettuccine or linguine with carrots, onion, broccoli, peas, and Alfredo sauce); stuffed shells; manicotti (stuffed with spinach and cheese); risotto Florentine (garlic, onion, cannellini beans, spinach, and parmesan); orzo risotto (rice and Parmesan); ziti with creamy Gorgonzola (Gorgonzola cheese, ziti, and Parmesan cheese).

Beans Italian white beans (great northern beans, sun-dried tomatoes, olives, basil and garlic); cannellini beans (white kidney beans mixed with pasta).

Meat and Fish Dishes Roast beef; pork medallions in creamy mushroom sauce; veal scallopine (mushroom sauce); veal Parmesan (bread-crumb batter, tomato sauce, and Parmesan cheese); turkey; pheasant; chicken cacciatore (mushrooms and olives); chicken marsala (marsala wine and mushrooms); chicken breasts stuffed with mozzarella, spinach, pesto, breading, and hazelnuts; broiled or grilled chicken with pesto, capers, and tomatoes; sautéed chicken breast piccada; fish alla Milanese (breaded flounder or haddock); shrimp scampi; shrimp marinara (tomato sauce, served over pasta or rice); squid stuffed with bread crumbs, walnuts, and garlic; octopus sautééd with tomatoes and red wine; grilled octopus (with garlic, olive oil, and lemon juice); stir-fried squid (with basil and garlic); Italian sausage; meatballs; braciola (beef rolls).

Desserts **Italian cookies** such as pignoli, biscotti, ring cookie, coconut macaroon, regina, centers, long John, quorsemali, musticiolli, bruti e buono, sfogliadelli, imbutitti, pasticiottini, amaretta, almond amaretta, torrone, cutout, filbert, truffles; **Italian**

Knowing Your Italian Foods

Types of Pasta

Farfalle or tripolini—bow tie
Fettuccine—long and flat
Fusilli—spring-shaped
Lasagna—flat and wide
Linguine—long, flat, and thin, and half the width of fettuccine
Macaroni—short, curved tube
Mafalda—mini lasagna
Manicotti or cannelloni—large, hollow tube
Mostaccioli—short diagonal macaroni with grooves
Penne—narrow tubes with or without grooves
Ravioli—square for filling
Rigatoni—short and wide with grooves
Rotelli—wide and short springs
Spaghetti—long, thin, and solid
Tortellini—small squares, filled and folded

Commonly Used Italian Herbs, Spices, and Flavor Enhancers

Basil—spicy, distinctive green herb, sweet with clovelike, pungent tang
Garlic—strong, pungent aroma and flavor (used extensively in Italian cooking)
Oregano—dried, green leaf, strong, aromatic with pleasantly bitter undertone
Parsley—slightly peppery leaves
Rosemary—aromatic green needles with fresh, sweet flavor

Saffron—distinctive, softly bitter
Sage—aromatic, slightly bitter leaves rubbed, ground

Cheeses and Their Flavors

Parmesan—piquant, sharp, very hard
Romano—piquant, sharp, very hard
Mozzarella—mild, semi-soft
Mascarpone—mild, creamy
Provolone—mild to sharp, smoky, semi-soft
Ricotta—mild and soft

For More Flavor

Olives
Olive Oil
Peppers
Onions
Capers

Pastries such as cannolli (custard-filled pastry), apricot puff pastry, Napoleon (puff pastry topped with fondant), Parmesan and cheddar cheese twist, cinnamon twist, apple and cream-filled pastry, croissant, panettone rolls, Italian scones (with candied fruits, raisins, and fennel seeds); **Cakes and pies** such as cornmeal-almond cake, mini-bundt cakes, apricot almond-cream tart with blackberries, cheesecake, spuma cioccolato (chocolate mousse cake, ladyfingers soaked in espresso and rum, with mascarpone and cocoa), torta carota (moist carrot cake with walnuts and butter-cream frosting); torta cioccolato (chocolate cake with chocolate glaze), tortas, tiramisu; **Italian candy**; **wanda**; **and frozen treats** including gelato, spumoni, Italian ice, sorbet, granita (Italian sorbet); panna cotta (an Italian eggless custard).

A Culinary Adventure Through Italy

Everyone knows something about Italian food. There are millions of restaurants worldwide dedicated to Italian cuisine. And just about everyone has a favorite Italian restaurant. Some common dishes we all know and love include pizza, spaghetti, ravioli, garlic bread, and all types of pastas with tomato-based sauces. Some common ingredients found in Italian dishes include garlic, olives and olive oil, tomatoes, and Parmesan cheese, as these are staples found all over Italy. Then there are ingredients and dishes that are specific to the various regions of Italy.

In this section, we will look at examples of dishes from various Italian regions to use for planning your Italian wedding menu. You may find that you prefer the foods of a certain region, or an appetizer from one, a main course from another, and a side dish from yet another. Feel free to mix and match the cuisines of the different regions.

The Foods of Northeast Italy

The **Northeast** region of Italy includes **Venice** and **Milan**. Here you will find meals prepared with lots of fresh fish and seafood, as well as seasonal produce like peas, zucchini, and asparagus. Meats, cheeses, polenta, and risotto are also incorporated into meals. A Northeastern antipasto might consist of a mixed seafood platter with crab, shrimp, mussels, squid, scallops, and red mullet, all accented with lemon juice and olive oil. A common side dish might be carpaccio, thin slices of raw beef served on arugula leaves and topped with Parmesan cheese and drizzled with olive oil. Another dish is suppa di cozze, mussels with white wine sauce, garlic, and parsley. Popular desserts here include tiramisu and gelato (ice cream).

Venice specializes in seafood, with exotic ingredients like pomegranate, pine nuts, and raisins. Also found here are creamy risottos with a seafood base, peas, spinach, asparagus, pumpkin, red-leaf raddichio, lots of pork dishes, heavy soups of beans, rice, and root vegetables. You will also find gnocchi with sweet-sour sauce, sweets and pastries like the thin oval biscuits called baicoli, ring-shaped cinnamon-flavored bussolai, and mandolato, which is a cross between nougat and toffee and is made with almonds.

Milan is known for its risotto alla Milanese, which is a saffron rice dish, sometimes cooked with the juices of roasted veal flavored with sage and rosemary. Milan also features osso bucco (shin of veal) biscotti flavored with nuts, vanilla, and lemon, and panettone, a soft egg cake with sultanas.

The Foods of Northwest Italy

Northwest Italy, which includes **Lombardy** and **Liguria**, features food that is rich and hearty and often cooked in lots of butter. Typical of Northwestern cuisine are risotto, various cheeses, truffles, and nuts, as well as grissini, crisp breadsticks that are served with most meals. In addition, foods are often prepared with garlic, saffron, basil, and wine. A Northwestern dish is bresaola, which consists of thin slices of cured raw beef with lemon and olive oil, served with farinata flat bread. For an appetizer, you might serve a vegetable tray with red, green, orange, and yellow peppers, celery, and scallions, served with anchovy dip. Other items from this region include an onion and herb focaccia, lean beef, veal, stuffed pheasant, mixed seafood, and chicken with tomato sauce. Desserts include amaretti, which are biscuits eaten with coffee; zabaglione, made with lady fingers; panettone, a light yeast cake with candied fruit; and torta di nocciole, a nut tart with hazelnuts.

The **Lombardy** region tends to be more rustic and features lots of risottos, polenta, and pizzocheri, which are buckwheat noodles found in the Valtellina Valley.

Liguria is well known for pesto, made with basil, pine nuts, oil and peccorino or Parmesan, served over pasta, often flat trenette noodles, or potato-based trofie. It is also used in soups like minestrone alla Genovese, pasta with various fish and seafood sauces. Liguria features fish soups and stews, such as ciupin, burrida di seppie (cuttlefish stew), and fish in carpione (marinated in vinegar and herbs). Some other dishes include cima alla Genovese (cold stuffed veal), torta pasqualina, which is a spinach and cheese pie, and foccaccia bread, often flavored with olives, sage, or rosemary. In this region, chickpeas grow abundantly along the coast and are used in zuppa de ceci, eggs, and farinata, a chickpea pancake. The city of Genoa is famous for its pandolce, a sweet bread with dried fruit and nuts.

The Foods of Central Italy

Central Italy includes **Florence, Tuscany, Umbria,** and **Le Marche**. Recipes of this region utilize olive oil, tomatoes, beans, hams, salami, and Parmesan. Dishes include an appetizer platter with various meats and ham; tortelloni (a large version of tortellini) stuffed with meat and cheese and served with a rich sauce; spaghetti al ragu, a traditional dish from Bologna, which is pasta topped with a generous portion of beef and tomato sauce; cannelloni, or large pasta tubes stuffed with meat or cheese; and steak and cod dishes. For dessert, Central Italy boasts torta di limone, a rich lemon dessert; panforte, which is a dense, dark cake spiced with cinnamon and cloves; and cantucci, sweet Tuscan biscuits.

Tuscany uses meat in many of its dishes. From the city of Florence comes bistecca alla Fiorentina, a char-grilled steak; arista, a roast pork loin stuffed with rosemary and garlic; and pollo alla diavola, chicken that is flattened, marinated, and then grilled with herbs. Olive oil is the essential flavoring of Tuscany, used as a dressing for salads, a medium for frying, and to pour over bread or vegetables and into soups and stews just before serving. Tuscan meals feature lots of soups, from vegetable broths to thick bean minestrone, and cannellini and borlotti beans in salads, with pasta (tuoni e lampo), or by themselves with a splash of olive oil.

Chickpeas are used in torta do ceci, and spinach is combined with ricotta to make gnocchi. The most popular cheeses of Tuscany are peccorino, which is made from sheep's milk, and marzolino from the Chianti region, eaten fresh or ripened. Desserts include cantuccini, which are hard, almond-flavored biscuits that are dipped into a glass of vin santo, and a host of sweet treats from the city of Siena, such as almond macaroons and panforte di Siena, a rich, sticky, nougat-like confection.

The Foods of Rome and Lazio

Menus from the **Rome** and **Lazio** region feature fresh produce, mushrooms, artichokes, and salad. Dishes are often seasoned with onions, garlic, rosemary, sage, bay leaves, sheep's milk cheese, and ricotta. A great antipasto from this region features batter-fried artichoke hearts and zucchini flowers. Some side or starter dishes include stracciatella, a soup with eggs, Parmesan cheese, and parsley; suppli di riso, which is fried rice croquettes stuffed with mozzarella; small potato or semolina dumplings served with tomato sauce or in butter; gnocchi alla Romana and risotto alla Romana, a rice dish made with a sauce of liver and sweet breads. For a main course, filetti di baccalá, deep-fried cod fillets, tender veal scalope cooked with ham, and veal involtini are favorites. Also from this region come fave al guanciale, young spring fava beans simmered in olive oil with pig's cheek and onion.

For dessert, try torta di ricotta, cheesecake filled with ricotta, marsala, and lemon. Coffee is almost more important to Roman life than wine, and espresso, cappuccino, and caffe latte are popular for different times of the day.

The Foods of Southern Italy

Southern Italy includes **Naples, Campania, Abruzzo, Molise, Puglia, Basilicate, Calabria, Sicily,** and **Sardinia.** The foods from the Southern region of Italy vary greatly according to each city. In Naples, a wafer-thin pizza is served. Sicilian food is rustic and voluptuous. Across the South, the dishes feature seafood, fruity green olive oil, dry white wine, fresh green vegetables, and large tomatoes. Southern Italy features one of the most healthy diets in Europe. Some of Italy's best olives are here. Dishes include grilled swordfish, squid, anchovies, shrimp, grilled tuna, lobster, and mussels; pizza Napolitana, a thin pizza topped with tomato, garlic, basil, and anchovies; sliced vegetables brushed with olive oil; lightly grilled zucchini and eggplant; marinated artichoke hearts; pesce spada, which is a swordfish steak; agnello arrosto, a juicy roast lamb; and southern cheeses, including provolone, ricotta, mozzarella, and scamorzo. Typical Southern seasonings are aromatic herbs such as rosemary, oregano, capers, sardines, sun-dried tomatoes, basil, mint, sage, thyme, and anchovies. Some of the finest olive oils in Italy (extra virgin) come from the South.

For dessert, consider Sicilian cassata, an ice cream made with ricotta cheese, candied fruit, pistachios, sugar, and chocolate in a sponge cake. Or try nougat, a sweet Sardinian specialty that can be made with nuts, or flavored with chocolate. Favorites also include cannoli and Sicilian almond bisuits.

Food in **Naples** is simple, with such favorites as Neapolitan pizza, also called Margherita, which features a simple tomato sauce, mozzarella cheese, and fresh basil on a thin crust. Popular dishes include spaghetti alle vongole; pasta e fagiole; broad bean or fresh pea soups; fried calamari; eggplant in red sauce; polpette di baccalá (small balls of minced salt-cod, fried or served in a fresh tomato sauce); cassuola di pesce (fish casserole); crocchette (potato croquettes with mozzarella cheese); linguine al cartoccio (seafood pasta made into a foil parcel and baked in the oven); and seafood pizza. Salads are often enhanced with fresh mozzarella. Sauces feature the region's prized tomatoes and a wide variety of ingredients, including hot peppers, veal shank, and a full bouquet of spices. And for dessert—gelato.

The southern region of **Puglia** boasts recipes made with fish from Bari, mussels from Tàranto, and pork, rabbit, and lamb from the inland hill towns. The national dish of Puglia is fave e cicoria, a purée of dry fava beans served with sautéed wild chicory. Strong-flavored ricotta forte is used in the sauces with the local pasta, orecchiette. A favorite regional cheese is burrate, a tear-shaped mozzarella shell filled with a heart of shredded mozzarella and cream. Puglia grows some of the best almonds in the word, which are used in many desserts and cookies

Sicily, a large island off the toe of the Italy boot, features a cuisine rich with seafood and cheeses. Some dishes include orange salads, couscous, rice balls, potato croquettes, fritters and small pizzas, rice, sardines, tuna and swordfish, and spaghetti can le sarde (pasta with seafood). Sicily features a variety of cheeses, including pecorino, provolone, caciocavallo, and sheep's-milk ricotta, which goes into many sweet dishes. And speaking of sweets, Sicily is famous for such treats as the rich cassata ice cream cake dish and cannoli.

Sardinia, a smaller island off Italy's mainland, offers a menu overflowing with fish and seafood, especially lobster grilled over open fires, scented with myrtle and juniper. Also common are suckling pig, prosciutto di conghiale, and ham. Some dishes from here include Spanish-inspired fish stews, botarga, which is a caviar made with mullet eggs; and a wide variety of pasta. You will find large ravioli filled with cheese and egg and maloreddus, which is similar to gnocchi but flavored with saffron. Also popular are cheeses made from ewe's milk, delicious breads—from carta da musica wafers to chunky rustic loaves—and lots of light and airy pastries, often flavored with lemon, almonds, or orange flower water.

Give Your Guests a Taste of all of Italy

For ultra decadence, consider setting up food stations, one for each region of Italy. If you plan to have a buffet-style meal, tables can be set up apart from each other, each one representing the foods from a particular region. This setup could be for appetizers only, for the entire meal, or for desserts. For example, during cocktail hour, feature an antipasto table with a tray from each region, clearly marked with signs "Northeast Italy," "Central Italy," and so on, one with cold seafood trays, one with an assortment of vegetables and another with cold meats and cheeses.

Combining Foods From Different Regions

When planning your wedding menu, you may choose foods from a particular region based on your heritage or preferences. Or, you might decide to combine the cuisines of various Italian locations. For example, you could serve a Northern Italian seafood antipasto along with fried calamari from Naples. Then, try risotto alla Milanese, a saffron rice dish from Milan, or stuffed cannelloni from Central Italy with a Northwestern onion-and-herb focaccia bread. For a main dish, opt for a Southern Italian grilled swordfish, zucchini, and eggplant, a Tuscan roast pork loin stuffed with rosemary and garlic, or a Roman veal scalòppa. Finally for dessert you could choose a Northeastern tiramisu with gelato, ice cream from Naples, and Sicilian cannolis.

The menu options are endless. You can mix and match Italian dishes however you like, and it will be a success. Choose a caterer who specializes in the type of foods you prefer or one who can prepare foods from various regions.

Dessert Station

A table filled with sweet delights, such as a basket of fresh fruits, trays of Italian cookies, pastries, biscotti, anise, and Italian ice cream makes a stunning feature. An array of fruit-flavored sorbets—coconut, mango, watermelon, pineapple, and pear—could be included, all served in the appropriate wrapping. For example, coconut sorbet could be served in a coconut shell, pear sorbet in a hollowed-out pear, and pineapple sorbet in a pineapple husk.

Wedding Cake

The wedding cake is an important part of the Italian wedding tradition. In the old days, the wedding cake was a symbol of fertility. The Romans made cakes out of wheat and would break them over the bride's head to ensure many children. Also, the Romans would eat cakes made of flour, salt, and water during the wedding ceremony, believing this would bring good luck to the couple.

Throughout the years, the wedding cake tradition evolved further. Small round cakes were stacked and the bride and groom would kiss over them for good luck. Then, bakers started decorating these stacked cakes with icing, small toys, and other decorative items. In the present, wedding cakes have become delicious works of art, available in more flavors, shapes, sizes, and designs than were ever thought possible back in the days of wheat, flour, salt, and water.

Wedding cakes at Italian weddings now are often very large and elaborate creations, which can serve as the focal point of the room and celebration. The cakes are often made up of several different recipes often featuring five or more layers—or separate rounds. One layer could be rum cake, while another might be strawberry shortcake with fresh strawberries inside, and yet another kiwi or lemon cake.

There is also a recipe in chapter 14 for Italian Wedding Cake, which is made with eggs, buttermilk, vanilla, and sometimes coconut and walnuts, and a cream cheese icing.

In addition to what's inside your wedding cake, you'll want to consider the outside. There are many choices when it comes to how you want your cake to look. You might consider a cake that fits the rest of your wedding theme—color scheme, style, formality, flower selections, and scenery/décor (which we'll see in chapter 11). Look through bakery catalogs and wedding magazines for ideas, and ask the baker for recommendations based on your preferences.

When looking for a good baker for your wedding cake, consider an Italian bakery, which may specialize in traditional Italian wedding cakes. Or you might find a caterer who also makes great wedding cakes. Look around and sample several bakeries before you decide.

Also consider giving the baker a special family recipe to follow for one of the cake layers. Perhaps you have a recipe in your family for an excellent rum cake, or a version of the Italian Wedding Cake you'd like to try. You can ask your baker to make a sample of the recipe for you to try ahead of time. Not only will it be a delicious addition to your wedding day, but a meaningful one as well. You can let guests know they are eating a cake recipe that was passed down from your Italian ancestors. Include printouts of the recipe with the slices of cake.

Wedding Cake Alternatives

Have a wedding cake made that looks like the leaning tower of Pisa. Because this Italian landmark already somewhat resembles a wedding cake with its eight layers stacked on top of each other, a sweet baked version isn't such a far-fetched idea. Eight layers of cake getting gradually thinner as they go up can be decorated with white, off-white, or gray-tinted frosting with designs resembling arches and columns around it and a flag on top. Of course the whole thing would be leaning slightly to one side.

For an alternative to a wedding cake, you might consider a tiered display of Italian pastries, cookies, and candies (you can do this in addition to a wedding cake), or cupcakes with little flags of Italy on them. The cupcakes could be made of the various recipes used in wedding cakes, such as rum cake and different fruits. Or have an ice cream cake with spumoni inside.

Cake Toppers

It has been traditional at Italian weddings to feature little smiling bride and groom figurines on the top of the wedding cake. These days you can find an extensive assortment of these miniature cake people or have them custom-made as you desire. Some companies will make tiny ceramic versions of the bride and groom, down to such details as hairstyles, facial expressions, and the style of the gown and tux.

You can also find clear glass, clay caricature, edible, and wire art deco versions. Or you can top your wedding cake with ceramic doves, wedding bells, or an item that is meaningful to you. Fresh flowers, fruit, or candy are more options.

For an Italian effect, you could top your cake with a custom-made bride and groom in a gondola. Or you can add a quirky touch with a miniature replica of the leaning tower of Pisa, the statue of David, or an Italian flag. You might also decorate the wedding cake with grapes, vines, and leaves, topping it off with bunches of grapes cascading down.

Wedding Cake Presentation

You may choose to have the cake proudly displayed in a visible spot, tucked away discreetly in a corner, or off by itself in a completely separate room until it's time to have the cake paraded out to the middle of the dance floor at a designated "cake cutting" time.

Italian Wedding Wines

Wine is a staple at Italian weddings, and the most important thing about wine at an Italian wedding is that there is lots of it. At most Italian weddings, wine is served with dinner, with bottles of red and white at every table.

When choosing the wine to serve at your wedding, take into consideration what you prefer and what you think your guests will like. You may have a favorite wine that you want to feature, or you may be open to different varieties. While you can choose wines from anywhere, featuring Italian wines is a nice touch. Italy not only produces and exports more wine than any other country, but it also offers the greatest variety of types with just about every color, style, and flavor you can imagine. Plus, many of these varieties are readily available from local distributors.

You may decide to taste some Italian wines prior to the wedding if you don't already have a preference, or you might trust your caterer to choose the wine for you.

When looking into Italian wines, consider the regions from which they come. While much of Italy produces great wines, they can vary greatly based on where the grapes were grown.

Wines From Different Regions

Northeast Italy, specifically the Veneto region, produces large amounts of everyday red, white, and rosé wines. In Northwest Italy, the Nebbiolo grape is used to produce two of Italy's finest red wines, Barolo and Barbaresco. Another Peidmont specialty is sparking Spumante.

Central Italy features the Sangiovese grape, which is the main grape in Chianti. This region also brings great varieties of Chardonnay and Cabernet Sauvignon. From Rome and Lazio comes Frascati, the best-known local white. Southern Italy produces more wine than any other region of Italy, with such producers as Regaleali, Rapitalà, Corvo, and Sicily's Marsala.

Among the best wines in Italy are Amarone, Barbaresco, Barolo, Brunello di Montalcino, Chianti, and Vino Nobile di Montepulciano.

A Wine Tour Through Italy

Northeast Italy Wines (Includes the Veneto and Friuli; Trentino-Alto Adige)

The **Veneto** region in Northeast Italy is considered a leader in the production and distribution of various wines. Here we find reds and whites, as well as some sparkling wines, with nutty, fruity, and occasionally bitter flavors. Two great wines from the Veneto region are Valpolicella and Bardolino. Valpolicella is a dry, light-to-medium-bodied wine that is best when consumed within four to five years. It is made from a blend of Corvina, Rondinella, and Molinara grapes. This hearty wine is also produced into a rich and dry Amarone della Valpolicella and a sweet Recioto della Valpolicella. Bardolino wine is very light-bodied and slightly darker than a rosé. It has a dry, crisp, warm flavor and is best consumed within three years of the vintage. Bardolino uses the same grapes as Valpolicella and comes in light red and dark pink chiaretto versions.

Other reds from the Veneto regions include Merlot, Cabernet, Schiopettino, the local red Raboso, the light and easy Cabernet Fran, which is sometimes mixed with Cabernet Sauvignon and aged in small oak barrels for more intense flavor. Amarone (or Amarone della Valpolicella) is a soft, dry red wine that can be aged for a long time.

White wines from the Veneto region include Soave, which is the most popular of Italian dry white wines. Others are the sweet Torcolato, Prosecco, which comes dry to softly sweet and slightly bubbly, the refined Superiore di Cartizze, Verduzzo, Pinot Grigio, Sauvignon Blanc, and Chardonnay.

Trentino–Alto Adige is Italy's northernmost region with Alpine borders on Austria and Switzerland and is split into two distinct provinces: Trentino to the south and Alto to the north. This region's best-known wines are the light to bright reds, such as Caldaro or Kalteresee, rosé Lagrein Kretzer, and the sweet dessert wine Moscato Rosa, with its flowery aroma. White wines include the aromatic Gewurztraminer, Sylvaner, Muller, Thurgau, and white Moscato. Also found here are

Chardonnay, Pinot Bianco, Grigio, Sauvignon, Riesling Renano, and the popular Pinot Grigio.

From **Trentino** comes the dry white Nosiola, which is also the base of the dessert wine vino santo.

Alto Adige produces a wide variety of table wines, which are light and extremely fresh, high-quality wines that do not need to be aged long.

Emilia-Romagna features two distinct parts. In Emilia, the western part of the region, the premier wine is Lambrusco, which ranges from purple to pink, and from sweet to dry. Albana di Romagna is a dry white wine that has a distinct almondy undertone. Sangiovese usually has a medium-bodied, fruity flavor that ends in a bitter bite. Also found here are Sauvignon, Chardonnay, the Pinots, and Cabernet.

Friuli Venezia Giulia features distinctive whites and attractive reds. The red wines include Merlot, Cabernet Sauvignon Grave, Cabernet Franc, Pinot Nero, and the native variety of Refosco, which can be made either light and fruity or into a durable wine for aging. Also found here is the blending of Cabernet Sauvignon, Merlot, and other varieties, aging the wine in small oak barrels. White wines from this region include the sweet Picolit, light dessert wines, and sparkling spumante.

Northwest Italy Wines (Includes Lombardy; Valle D'Aosta and Piedmont; Liguria)

Valle d'Aosta is Italy's smallest region in the mountainous northwestern corner against borders of Switzerland and France. Here, we find light reds and whites with delicate tastes and light flavors. The quality of the wines in this region is quite good; however they aren't always easy to find outside Italy.

Grape varieties range from Piedmontese (Nebbiolo, Dolcetto, Moscato) to French (Chardonnay, the Pinots, Gamay) to the teutonic Muller Thurgau. The most intriguing wines of this region are Petit Rouge of Enfer d'Arvier and Torrette, the Blanc de Valdigne of Morgex and La Salle, the Petite Arvine, and the Malvoisie.

Piedmont is home to some of the greatest unique red wine, like Barolo and Barbaresco and the best known white, sweet, bubbly—Asti Spumante and Moscato d'Asti. The red Barbaresco comes from the Nebbiolo grape and has a violet and vanilla scent, and a dry, warm, and tannic taste. Barolo, also from the Nebbiolo grape, is dry, full-bodied, austere, tannic, and sapid, and has a rose, violet, and licorice scent.

The wines from this region, dark reds, very light whites, and sparkling wines, are often chewy in substance and woody in taste, and are of very high quality.

Liguria produces dry white Cinqueterre, red and white Vermentino, red soft, fruity and full-flavored Rossese di Dolceacqua, red Ormeasco and Rossese di Albenga, and white Pigato and Vermentino.

Lombardy does not produce much wine. However, this region successfully grows the Nebiolo grape. Wines from here include reds like Grumello, Inferno, Sassella, Valgella, Villa dei Faglia, and Terra di Franciacorta, and the white variety Terre di Franciacorta.

Central Italy Wines (Includes Emilia-Romagna; Florence; Tuscany; Umbria; Le Marche)

Tuscany is the heartland of Italian winemaking and the home of Chianti. Made with the Sangiovese grape, Chianti is a very rich, dry, red wine with aromas of cherries and violets, flavors of tart cherries, and very high acidity. It can range from very light-bodied to intense and full-bodied. Some varieties include Chianti Classico, Chianti Classico Villa Antinori, Chianti Classico Villa Primavera, and Chianti Sigillo.

Other prime reds from Tuscany include Brunello di Montalcino and Vino Nobile di Monterpulciano, Rosso di Montalcino, and Santa Cristina. Brunello di Montalcino is made from the Sangiovese grape and ages at least four years in oak or chestnut barrels. It's a dark red wine with a dry, warm, full-bodied flavor and scent of blackberry and soft rose.

Tuscan white wines include Vernaccia di San Gimignano, Galestro, and vin santo, a sweet, strong dessert wine made from grapes left to dry in the sun.

Umbria produces two reds: Torgiano, a Sangiovese-based wine that is similar to Chianti, and a medium-bodied Sagratino di Montefalco. White wines from Umbria include the rich Brezza, Ovierto, Orvieto Classico, and Orvieto Classico Secco.

Emilia-Romagna brings us Lambrusco, which is well-known throughout the world, and is grapey, dry, bubbly, and goes with rich foods. Also from this region are red Cagnina di Romagna and Lambrusco di Modena.

Le Marche produces the white wine Verdicchio dei Castelli di Jesi.

Rome and Lazio Wines (Includes Rome and Lazio)

Lazio produces white wines Frascati Superiore and Est! Est! Est! di Monte-fiascone.

Southern Italy Wines (Includes Naples and Campania; Abruzzo, Molise, and Puglia; Basilicata and Calabria; Sicily; Sardinia)

Naples features a local white wine, Lacrima Christi, which means "tears of Christ."

Abruzzo produces simple wines at good values. Wines from this region include Montepulciano d'Abruzzo, a red wine that is low in tannin and acid and is easy to drink, and the white wine Trebbiano D'Abruzzo. The Monterpulciano grape variety is related and similar to the Sangiovese.

From **Campania** comes one of Italy's longest-lived red wines, Taurasi. It is made from the Aglianico grape variety (near Naples) and is full-bodied and tannic. A white wine from this region is Fiano di Avellino.

Puglia makes more wine than any other Italian region. The wines from here tend to be strong and full-bodied, and have enjoyed a good reputation since ancient times. Today there are about twenty-four different wines produced in Puglia—white, red, rosé, sparkling wine, and sweet Muscat. Its best known red wine is Salice Salentino, a warm, full-bodied, low-acid wine. Another popular and powerful red is Cacc'emmitte, from Foggia province. Other reds from this region are Aglianico, Rupicolo di Rivera, Salice Salentino Leone De Castris, and Donna Marzia. White wines include the light, delicate dry white Locorotondo and Agorà.

Sicily also produces a lot of wine, especially red. The wines from this region are flavorful and high-quality. Mainly associated with the fortified Marsala, the island also produces quality everyday wines, such as red Corvo and white Regaleali. The

Duca di Salaparuta winery makes Corvo and Duca Enrico, a rich full-bodied, concentrated red wine with an intense bouquet.

Vernaccia is the most famous **Sardinian** wine with a hearty flavor similar to sherry. It can range from a very dry version to a sweet variant as a dessert wine. Other Sardinian wines include Mandrolasi, an easy-drinking red, and Cannonau di Sardegna, a heady red wine. White wines are dry Torbato or the full-flavored Trebbiano Sardo.

Serving Wine at Your Wedding

In addition to serving wine with dinner, you might consider making wine an even bigger part of your wedding. Consider setting up wine stations, perhaps featuring wines from different regions, or having a wine tasting during the reception. This could take place during the cocktail hour or throughout the evening. Supply guests with a sheet listing the wines they are tasting and how they might acquire it later. For information on a wine-tasting wedding, see chapter 12.

Or, you might consider serving a different wine with every course. For example, you might start with a light white wine with appetizers, followed by a drier white during a first course, a red during the next course, and a dessert wine later. Include a menu card at each place setting listing the wine to be served with each course.

You may just keep each table supplied with a bottle of red and one of white to be drunk throughout the feast. Just make sure that servers replace the empty bottles as needed. Wine is part of the Italian wedding celebration and should flow freely.

Italian Wedding Liqueurs

Wine isn't the only beverage found in abundance at Italian weddings. Sweet and strong liqueurs are also frequently served. As mentioned in chapter 8, it has been customary at Italian weddings through the years for the best man to greet guests with drinks at the reception—offering sweet liqueurs to the ladies and strong drinks to the men. Feature these beverages during cocktail hour or throughout the celebration. Many of the sweet liqueurs can also be served as after-dinner drinks or with dessert.

The Sweet Liqueurs

Amaro—a bitter, after-dinner drink

Amaretto—much sweeter with a strong taste of almond; made from apricot pits

Anisette—fragrant with a sharp licorice taste; made from anise seeds

Crème de cacao—sweet, chocolate-flavored

Lemon liqueur—an Italian liqueur infused with fresh lemon peels and sweetened; it tastes like potent sweetened lemonade and is usually bottled at 30 percent alcohol; similar to a lower strength, but sweetened

Lemon-lime liqueur—an Italian sweet or semi-dry liqueur made with lemon and lime peels

Lime liqueur—an Italian or Mediterranean sweet or semi-dry liqueur made with lime peels or lime juice

Limoncello or limoncino—a lemon-based liqueur best sipped from a frozen, vase-shaped glass

Maraschino liqueur—a cordial from bitter wild cherry

Sambucca—an Italian sticky-sweet anise-flavored liqueur made from elderberries; traditionally served with a coffee bean in it and set on fire

Strega—sweet, yellow, herb-and-saffron based in tall bottles; one of the most popular liqueurs in Italy

Tuaca—an Italian sweet liqueur flavored with citrus

Other sweet liquors include Liquore Centerba, Centerba Toro, Limoncello di Sorrento, and Grappa Monovitigno.

Italian Wedding Strong Drinks

Brandy—produced from the juice of grapes, as well as other fruits

Cognac—a brandy distilled from grapes

Grappa—an Italian brandy made from distilling grape skins that remain after wine production

Whiskey—distilled from fermented grain; stored in oak containers

Mixed Drinks to Serve at Your Italian Wedding

You may decide to have a full-service bar at your wedding or you may limit drinks to beer and wine and perhaps include a few select hard and mixed drinks. Here are a few concoctions that have an Italian flavor, either in name or ingredients, which could be a fun addition to your selection.

Citrus Cooler—dark rum, triple sec, sweet and sour mix, lime juice, and lemon-lime soda

Pink Lemonade—rum, club soda, cranberry juice, and lemon juice

Godfather—Scotch and amaretto

Summer Lemonade—vodka, orange curaçao, sweet and sour mix, and lemon-lime soda

Champagne Punch—champagne, cognac, cherry liqueur, Triplesec, lemon juice, and simple syrup

Italian Stinger—cognac and Galliano over ice in an old-fashioned glass

Angel's Tip—dark crème de cacao and half-and-half

Amaretto Spritzer—amaretto and club soda

Wedding Cake—amaretto, crème de cacao, and milk, served in a chilled champagne glass or over ice

Fino Martini—gin and fino sherry

Napoleon—gin, white curaçao, Dubonnet

Renaissance—gin, fino sherry, and half-and-half

Roman Cooler—gin, punt e mes, lemon juice, sweet vermouth, simple syrup, and sparking water

Italian Wedding Coffees

Coffee is a big part of Italian life, and therefore it is an absolute must at an Italian wedding. It is usually made available throughout the entire reception, but especially after dinner and during dessert. In addition to serving regular and decaffeinated blends with cream and sugar, espresso and cappuccino can be featured.

Consider having an Italian coffee and cordial table set up at dessert time. Feature several types of coffee—regular, decaf, flavored—as well as espresso and cappuccino, along with grappa, anisette, amaretto, and crème de cacao. Tea, lemon, sugar, cinnamon, sweeteners, cream, milk, and half-and-half could also be included.

Choosing a Caterer

Because food is such an important part of any wedding, especially an Italian wedding, choosing a good caterer is a major, and perhaps the most important, wedding planning decision you will make.

The location you have chosen for your reception might include a caterer, especially if it is an Italian restaurant. However, if your reception is being held at a site that includes its own catering but the meal selections do not include Italian food, you will want to ask if you can bring in your own caterer. Some venues allow this; some do not. Others will allow it with limitations, such as providing a list of other caterers to choose from. If having an Italian feast is important to you, this is something you'll want to clear up early on in the planning process.

Assuming you are free to hire any caterer you choose, not provided by the reception location, where do you start? You may already know a great Italian caterer who you plan to hire. Maybe a friend of the family, even a relative who provides feasts for huge events, or a favorite Italian restaurant that you know will do a great job. Or, you may have been to an Italian wedding that had great food, and you can hire the same caterer.

For my own Italian wedding, choosing the caterer was easy. My husband and I knew we wanted our favorite little family-owned-and-run restaurant, Bella Italia, to feed our guests the way they stuffed us with home-cooked delights so many times. Plus, we had eaten there so often they had become our friends and like our family. And, as we know, good friends and family are right up there with the food on the list of most important aspects of Italian weddings. Someone we knew and liked would be perfect. And we trusted them to do a great job—their food is excellent, they keep the wine flowing, they're warm, friendly, and outgoing, and they always go that extra mile to serve their guests well. Plus, the owner sings Italian songs to a karaoke machine every night. They catered our wedding—with appetizers, antipasto, salad, focaccia bread, stuffed chicken, manicotti, and Italian sausage—and served wonderful food just like we knew they would.

The best way to decide on the right caterer for your Italian wedding is to trust your own instincts, tastes, and appetite, as well as word of mouth and track record.

If you don't have a favorite Italian restaurant, ask around. Then try as many restaurant/caterers as you can until you find that perfect one for your wedding. Find out all you can from them, such as whether they've catered Italian weddings before, how many, what size, and if you can talk to someone whose wedding they have catered.

Then discuss every detail with them, including but not limited to the following: the number of guests you're inviting and they can accommodate; the date, time, location, and whether they're available; the number of courses; specific dishes; if they will include appetizers, desserts, beverages, coffee; how many servers they'll provide; will the food be cooked ahead of time or at the location; cooking devices, outlets, hook-ups, kitchen space needed and so on; what they will bring and what you will need to supply, such as warming trays, dishes, silverware, glasses, coffee cups, coffee, creamers and sugar bowls, coffeemakers, tablecloths and napkins, salt and pepper shakers; the price with tax; and amount of deposit. Be sure to get everything in writing.

Another consideration when planning your wedding feast is how it will be served. Will it be buffet-style or delivered to the tables by food servers? Think about the logistics of each and which will best suit your needs and preferences.

Will each plate be made up before it's brought to the tables, or will platters be brought for guests to pass around family-style, taking their own servings? If buffet-style, how will food stations be set up and how will guests line up to get their food? Will someone go around to each table letting them know it's their turn? Will they bring their plates from the tables or pick them up at food stations? If the meal is served while guests are seated, you might have buffet-style for appetizers and desserts.

When deciding whether to have buffet or sit-down, also take into consideration the size and setup of your reception site, kitchen space for food preparation, who the servers will be and how many will be needed, and where electrical outlets are located.

Once you've chosen a caterer and come to an agreement on all the practicalities, together you can plan the menu. You might have a distinct menu in mind or you may want the caterer to help you decide. Likely you will both have suggestions. Your menu options are unlimited and you are sure to have fun deciding.

A Sample Italian Wedding Menu

When guests arrive, they are served a choice of a Godfather or champagne punch (see above) or beer, wine, or a soft drink. After a brief welcome by the best man, the guests are free to graze on appetizers and antipasto, which include:

Fried calamari, zucchini, and mozzarella; vegetable trays; shrimp cocktail; deep dish pizza; and an antipasto platter of salami, prosciutto, mozzarella, provolone, peppers, olives, and marinated artichoke hearts.

After guests take their seats, they toast the bride and groom with Asti Spumante.

Next, the meal begins with a mixed green and tomato salad with a vinaigrette, followed by minestrone and garlic bread, pasta primavera, a choice of chicken cacciatore or veal scallopine, and eggplant Parmesan and meatballs. Chianti is the wine of choice, while Chardonnay is also available.

For dessert, guests are offered slices of wedding cake, made from a family recipe for rum cake, along with selections from a dessert table, including cannolis, assorted Italian cookies, and a scoop of spumoni. Coffee, espresso, and anisette are also served.

Menu Selection Worksheet

Who the caterer will be:

Buffet or sit-down:

Number of courses to be served (three, seven, fourteen?):

Antipasto:

Other appetizers:

Salad:

Soup:

Bread:

Pasta course:

Meats (roast beef, pork, pheasant, turkey, chicken, veal, fish, seafood):

Hot dishes (eggplant, sausage and peppers, meatballs, vegetables, sides):

Cold dishes (roast pepper salad, fresh fruit, pickled eggplant):

Wedding cake:

Dessert (Italian pastries, cakes, pies, cookies, candies, ice creams):

Wine:

Champagne:

Other beverages:

Coffees and cordials:

10

Italian Wedding Music and Dances

As Shakespeare said, "if music be the food of love, play on!" and Italian events are planned with lots of music, food, and love. At the traditional Italian wedding, you will never find any of the three lacking. We've already discussed the importance of food at the elaborate celebration, and the love is apparent in the newlyweds and the closeness of the families and friends.

So now, we turn our attention to the music. And where there is music, there is sure to be dancing—sometimes until the break of dawn. At most Italian weddings, music and traditional dances continue throughout the celebration, from the time guests enter the church to the last dance. The forms of music played are endless: soft classical, festive folk, modern-day pop, rock, and then some. Sources range from one to four musicians playing string and wind instruments, operatic soloists and choirs, to several-member bands and DJs playing recorded music.

In this chapter we will look at the role of music and dance in Italian culture, especially when it comes to weddings. We will explore the many options available when it comes to Italian wedding music, for songs played during the ceremony, cocktail hour, dinner, and dancing. We will also explore the various traditional Italian wedding dances, including the waltz, polka, and the Tarantella.

The Importance of Music in the Wedding Celebration

Think of any passionate or romantic scene from the movies. It's more than likely that you can remember the music that accompanied it. Music dramatically sets the tone and the mood, builds excitement, and enhances celebrations, making them more meaningful, memorable, and enjoyable. Consider what kind of mood you'll be trying to set during different parts of your wedding celebration. You may want to use strictly traditional Italian music, or you might just want to add touches of it here and there.

Italian Music—Viva La Musica!

There is a full range of Italian music available, from the earliest forms of classical to modern-day classical, to opera, jazz, and dance music. There are festive instrumentals, like the many versions of the Tarantella, for dancing and clapping along. With their festive and catchy beats, many of these songs are easily recognizable as Italian.

Just as Italy is admired worldwide for its excellence in the visual arts—masterful paintings, sculpture, and architecture—it is renown for its long tradition in music. Some of the most brilliant music came from Italy, starting with the Gregorian chant, troubadour song and the madrigal, to classical and opera.

The music of Italy moved through the medieval and Renaissance period, where music was interconnected with dancing and poetry, and into the Baroque period, with small-scaled operas to classicism and then the full-scale modern opera. In fact, the very first operas were created as part of the wealthy wedding celebration. Later came contemporary music and music theater.

Many masters of music have come from Italy, from Antonio Vivaldi to Giuseppe Verdi, Domenico Scarlatti, Cimarosa, Donizetti, Bellini, Boito, and Puccini, to all three tenors (Luciano Pavarotti, José Carreras, and Placido Domingo).

Italian Styles of Music

Gregorian chant—choral melody introduced into the service of the Christian church by Pope Gregory I about the end of the sixth century.

Troubadour song—a song; trope; name given to a class of early poets who first appeared in France, and flourished from the eleventh to the latter part of the thirteenth centuries, their poetry being lyrical and amatory.

Madrigal—a vocal composition, now commonly consisting of two or more parts with five or six singers.

Opera—a musical drama; a dramatic composition set to music and sung and acted on the stage, accompanied by musical instruments; the score or words of a musical drama

Symphony—a harmony of sounds agreeable to the ear; an elaborate composition for a full orchestra, consisting usually of three or four contrasted but intimately related movements.

Music From Different Cities

Various parts of Italy are known for their own music traditions: Rome had very conservative beginnings; Venice cultivated religious music, and has since been credited for producing the music of love; Florence produced revived versions of ancient Greek music; and Milan became famous for opera. Sicilian music has mystic quarter tones more reminiscent of Greek music played on instruments like the guartara (a terra-cotta wind instrument), the ciaramedda (the shepherd's goatskin bagpipe), the friscaletta (reed flute), and the tamburedda (skin drum).

Great musical landmarks exist in Italy as well, such as Milan's La Scala opera house. In nearby Cremona, you can visit some of the greatest musical instruments in the world, as well as the tomb of violin producer Anthony Stradivari.

Choosing the Music for Your Italian Wedding

To choose the right music for your Italian wedding, consider the various parts of the celebration in which you would like to have music played: The ceremony, while guests are being seated, prelude, processional, songs during the service, interlude, and recessional; and the reception, for the receiving line, cocktail hour, dinner, and dancing.

You might choose to have a combination of live and recorded music played throughout your wedding. While your band or musicians might be able to perform a wide array of music, there may be certain songs you'd prefer to hear played by their original artists.

If you want to have a variety of Italian music played throughout your wedding, consider having your band, musicians, or DJ intersperse recorded music into the repertoire. Many great Italian music CDs can be found with songs perfect for different parts of your wedding. Played at just the right moment, these songs can add just the right Italian flavor. Look for albums by, or including songs from, Italian greats like Louis Prima, Dean Martin, Achille Togliani, Paolo Conte, Lou Monte, Al Martino, Julius La Rosa, Paul Anka, Jerry Vale, Mario Lanza, Vic Damone, Perry Como, and Connie Francis.

Some excellent CDs with assorted Italian music collections include *Italian Love Songs*, *Mob Hits*, *Now That's Italian: Original Hits by the Original Artists*, *Bravo Italia: We Three*, *Ciao Italia!: Italy's Greatest Hits*, *The Very Best of Lou Monte*, anything by Frank Sinatra, especially the soundtrack from *Mickey Blue Eyes*. Of course there are several more, which you can find at many music stores or via the Internet on such sites as Amazon.com. And don't forget to choose a special song for each of the following: the bride and groom's first dance; the father/daughter dance; the mother/son dance;

the bridal party dance; the cake cutting; the bouquet toss; the garter toss; the last dance of the evening; and the departure of the bride and groom.

Preparing for Dancing at the Wedding

The bride and groom might take some dance lessons prior to the wedding. There are many types of ballroom and other dancing lessons offered through professional dance companies, colleges, and city programs. You can enroll in a one- or two-time lesson or in a class that goes on for several months.

You might also have a dance party, where an instructor or very talented friend or relative teaches everyone the dances, especially if you find someone who knows the Tarantella. That way, your guests, or at least many of them, can all join in at the wedding. Another option is to have dance demonstrations or lessons at the wedding as part of the entertainment.

Traditional Italian Dances

A big part of a traditional Italian wedding are the cultural dances for which everyone kicks up their heels to the lively music. Young and old and everyone in between will usually jump up on the dance floor and demonstrate the moves they all know. And if they don't know all the moves, they still participate.

At most Italian weddings, a wide variety of dances are featured such as the Tarantella, the pizzica tarantata, tammurriata, Bal Del Truc, Ballo Sardo, Il Codiglione, La Lavandera, Quadriglia Di Aviano, La Raspa, Saltarello Di Romangna, the polka, waltz, chicken dance, conga line, mazurka, La Furlana, Istanpitta, St. Vitus Dance, and the Marcarena. There also may be fifteenth century Italian dances like Petite Riense, Anello, Geloxia, and Leoncello, and sixteenth century Contropasso, Fiamma d'Amore, Gracca Amoroso, and Barriera. Following is a rundown of some of these popular dances.

The Tarantella

Perhaps the best-known Italian dance is the Tarantella, which now has dozens of versions of music to accompany it. Every traditional Italian wedding should feature some aspect of the Tarantella; if not the dance itself, then at least the music.

The Tarantella is a lively and graceful folk dance that originated in Southern Italy and has become symbolic of "Mediterranean vitality." The name Tarantella is said to be influenced by the Lycosa tarantula, or Arania or Apulian spider. Some say that the Tarantella developed somewhere between the fifteenth and seventeenth centuries from tarantism, the disease caused by the spider's venomous bite. The pain from the bite was so intense it caused the victim to jump around spastically, as if he or she was dancing.

Another version of this belief was that a person bitten by the tarantula could be cured through frenzied dancing, which caused the poison to be sweated out. The townspeople would play music and the afflicted person would dance the venom away, and the dance sometimes lasted for days. It was later found that it wasn't actually the tarantula that was poisonous, but another spider.

Some say that the dance came from the towns of Toranto and Tarentum, where women who worked in the fields were often bitten by spiders and made to dance the poison out. To get the suffering victims to dance, people played the most upbeat music, with guitars and violins.

Still others believe that the Tarantella came about as a "courtship" dance, as the steps appear to express a young man's love for the girl he is dancing with.

Whatever the origin, during the nineteenth century the Tarantella developed into the colorful and popular dance that is still performed today at festivals, weddings, and celebrations of all kinds. In Salento, festivals often feature ceremonial and therapeutic music and dancing around bonfires for superstitious reasons. In Galantina (on the Salentine peninsula) everyone gathers on June 28 and 29 at the churches dedicated to Saints Peter and Paul in honor of their feast days and performs the Tarantella.

The Tarantella spread all over Europe in the form of ballets, such as "La Tarentule" in the nineteenth century, and as a dance performed in ballrooms. This dance that was originally reserved for the lower and middle classes had made its way up. The Tarantella was eventually condensed into eight steps and was danced by a group of three girls or by a couple. It came to be bad luck to dance the Tarantella alone.

The Tarantella is built in a six-eight measure and with a "abbastanza mosso tempo." It is a swift, whirling dance with light, quick steps and a "teasing" flirt. The dance starts with a jumping motion, has obvious signs of love and pleasure, and each gesture is made with grace and voluptuousness. It is performed by couples of dancers who play castanets, mandolins, or tambourines while dancing.

Often, three girls dance the Tarantella; one plays a tambourine while the other two step in time and spin around in place using castanets. The girls switch off with the tambourine so they can rest during this high-energy dance that can last for hours.

When the Tarantella is danced by a couple, it is a love story in motion. The woman uses her energy and swiftness to incite the love of her partner, while he tries to win her over with his liveliness and affection. Throughout the dance, they come together, part, unite, and leap into each other's arms. In their different gestures, they take turns teasing each other with affection and disinterest.

The dance starts out with the man kneeling while gazing at his partner as she dances for him. He then moves away from her as though no longer intrigued, but only temporarily. He moves about the dance floor, turning, begging, retreating, and skipping around. She plays her tambourine, swings her skirt, picking up the corners, raises her arms, and turns. They circle each other.

There are many ways to dance the Tarantella, but the most important or constant components are: it is danced as a group or as couples; women wear full skirts and pick up edges of their skirts and flourish them; instruments like tambourines and castanets often accompany the dance; it is fast-paced with lots of turns, skips, circling your partner, flirty gestures, and movement about the floor; and most important, it includes the lively music, which comes in different varieties, such as Tarantella (Basic), Tarantella Montevergine, Tarantella Napoletana, and Tarantella Siciliana. To include the Tarantella in your wedding, consider having a box of musical instruments on hand for guests to play on the dance floor. Note: to dance the Tarantella, all you really need to do is get out there and move to the music!

Polka

Another dance you will often see at Italian weddings is the polka. Although not originally a dance from Italy, the polka's lively tempo makes it a fun addition to the festive Italian wedding.

The polka is a folk dance that is said to have originated in Bohemia and became popular in various ballrooms in the mid-nineteenth century. Throughout the years, the polka made its way from Poland to London and then to Italy. Today it is a favorite dance of many cultures and is praised both for its intimacy and its vivacity.

The polka originally started out with frenzied hopping, but became more calm with rising and falling as the feet moved, with three steps and a hop to each bar of the music.

The polka is a spin-off of the waltz, and like its predecessor, is done in the "closed position," and is a round dance. In round dances, there is an element of push and pull, where one partner is pushed along the line of the dance. The polka consists of many half steps, or quick movements from one foot to the other and has a three-four time.

Waltz

The waltz is a great dance for the bride and groom to learn for their first dance. In this romantic dance, the man holds the woman close, as they swing and whirl around the room. This dance can range in tempo from fast to medium to slow. It starts with the couple standing next to one another, holding hands. They end up facing each other as they balance side to side and take turns following each other.

The Chicken Dance

Toward the latter part of the reception, many Italian weddings often feature the wildly fun Chicken Dance, which is easy to learn on the spot and allows everyone to participate. Once the familiar music begins, everybody knows what to do.

The bride, groom, and guests find a spot on the dance floor and do the simple motions: throw your hands up in the air and snap your fingers four times, put your hands under your arms and flap like a chicken four times, wiggle your hips four times, and then clap four times. You do this sequence four times and then the music changes and everyone skips around in circles, joining elbows.

Mazurka

Some Italian weddings feature the mazurka, which is similar to a waltz, only more complex. Originally from Poland, this dance features undulating and sideways gliding movements, which are done gracefully. The music is three-four or three-eight measure and was first composed by Markowsky.

Conga Line

The Conga line is a fun activity that often takes place at Italian weddings. Everyone lines up single file, with the bride in the lead, followed by the groom. With their hands on the hips or shoulders of the person in front of them, the group dances around as they begin to move forward. The steps often are a one-two-three and kick or bump. The line zigzags all over the dance floor, the room, and wherever else the bride takes it.

Macerana

Another simple dance that everyone can easily catch on to is the Macerana, which recently became popular at weddings and celebrations—Italian weddings included. Everyone stands on the dance floor facing the same way. The movements are: right arm out with palm facing down, left arm out palm down, right palm up, left palm up, right hand to left shoulder, left hand to right shoulder, right hand behind head, left hand behind head, right hand to left hip, left hand to right hip, then shake and sway hips. Do this whole progression three times and then jump one-quarter turn to the left and start again.

More Italian Dances

There are several other dances you might consider learning and incorporating into your Italian wedding. Following are a few more suggestions.

Minuet: called the Calata in Italy, it has small steps, is done around the room in a S or Z shape, and is simple, almost like walking.

Chacon: an Italian or Spanish folk dance, which is wild and sensual, using a lot of hip movements, and is often performed with tambourines and castanets.

Coranto: a dance from Italy with a rapid tempo that features skipping and zigzagging around the dance floor.

La Furlana: similar to the Tarantella, but not as diversified and more ragged. This dance was popular with the gondoliers in Venice. It came from the Friuli region of Italy and is still danced there.

Gagliarde: originated in Lombardy, in Northern Italy, it is a lively and romantic dance done in triple time, and features kicks with alternate legs and jumping in the air.

Other Italian Activities Involving Music

At many Italian weddings, music is used to engage the audience, even those who do not wish to get up out of their seats. While guests are seated for dinner, the song "Que Sera Sera, Whatever Will Be" may start playing, which will cause guests to swing their napkins around in circles above their heads and sing along.

Another simple activity calls for guests to flock to the dance floor and assemble into a large circle. "That's Amore" plays as everyone holds hands, swings hands up and down, and sings along. Right after that, "New York, New York" may begin to play and everyone, still singing along, might kick their legs out alternating, as in a kick line or kick circle.

Setting the Italian Wedding Stage

NOW THAT YOU'VE EXPLORED many of the elements that go into making a true Italian wedding—customs, food, and music, it's time to set the stage. When it comes to planning your Italian wedding setting—enhancing the location with flowers, colors, lighting, and decorations—the options are limitless.

But before you do anything, you must first decide where you will be holding your wedding ceremony and reception. Will your ceremony and reception be held at one location or at separate venues? Do you want to have an indoor or outdoor affair? Do you prefer a large church, small chapel, garden, hotel, banquet hall, restaurant, home, historic building, or some other venue?

Once you've chosen your site or sites, set the date and time, and determined an approximate number of guests and budget, you can start planning the ambience for your Italian wedding. This is your chance to really get creative and have some fun.

In this chapter, we will look at developing the ambience of your celebration— color scheme, flowers and other decorations, centerpieces and other props. Some of these decisions may have already been made based on your wedding wardrobe choices—the color of the bridesmaids' dresses and the flowers in the personal bouquets. However, you may choose to decorate the venue independent of these selections. Just because you use a certain type of flower for the bridal and bridesmaids' bouquets doesn't mean you have to use the same kind in your centerpieces and decorative floral arrangements. You are free to use whatever you choose.

Also in this chapter, we will also explore how to create various types of Italian-inspired settings. Tips, ideas, suggestions, and instructions for various props and special effects will be included. To get us in the mood, let's take a tour of the land we plan to emulate.

Slices of Italy

If you could capture the essence of Italy and transport it into your wedding setting, what would you include? What do you picture when you think of Italy? The art, the architecture, the beautiful landscape? A certain city, such as Milan, Palermo, or Venice? Or particular points of interest like the Vatican, the Spanish Steps, the Amalfi coast, or Tuscan vineyards? Do you envision a huge feast at a long banquet table with chalices and candelabras? A romantic gondola ride under bridges and stars? Sunshine, green meadows, quaint villas, and immense vineyards? Or cobblestone roads lined with little shops, restaurants, and cafés?

When considering the sights of Italy, there are numerous images that come to mind. Spectacular landscaping is everywhere. The wide array of scenery includes vast countryside, rolling hills, and an assortment of breathtaking coastlines. The various floral regions of Italy carry various types of trees and vegetation. The Alpine region features oaks, chestnuts, beeches, firs, larches, and Scotch pines. The summit areas contain meadows, pastures, and shrub vegetation. An Apennine region features conifers, and a Po region contains willows, alders, poplars, oaks, American acacias, heather, and broom. Finally, a Mediterranean region combines a mixture of maritime pine, evergreen, olives, cypresses, and corks. Many of these natural resources can be added to your wedding décor.

Italy is known for its impressive art and literature. Picture baroque artwork—highly ornate paintings, sculptures, and fountains—and amazing architecture. Italy is filled with world-renowned museums housing the creations of the masters, and is admired for its one-of-a-kind buildings.

Grapes, vineyards, wineries, and quaint villas and cafés are all found throughout Italy and feature prominently in Italian imagery.

When it comes to decorating your Italian wedding panorama, you have many options. You can incorporate subtle hints here and there to achieve an Italian flavor, or you can go all out and re-create your own Little Italy. You might utilize props and décor that represent Italy in general, or ones that are native to specific cities or regions. Combing various elements of national, regional, and local Italian features is great fun and makes for a stunning atmosphere. Before you begin rebuilding Rome or Sicily, let's take a mini tour through Italy and its various regions and cities.

Italian Cities and Regions

In addition to the resources that represent Italy as a whole, the various cities and regions within the country have their own unique characteristics. You may decide to accentuate one region over another, or you may want to incorporate features from each.

Valle d'Aosta: Aosta
Piedmont: Turin, Alessandria, Asti, Biella, Cuneo, Novara, Verbania, Vercelli
Liguria: Genoa, Imperia, La Spezia, Savona
Lombardy and the Lakes: Milan, Bergamo, Brescia, Como, Cremona, Lecco, Lodi, Mantova, Mantua, Pavia, Sondrio, Varise
Veneto: Venice, San Marco, Belluno, Padua, Rovigo, Treviso, Verona, Vicenza
Trentino-Alto Adige: Trento, Bolzano

Friuli-Venezia Giulia: Trieste, Gorizia, Pordenome, Udine

Emilia-Romagna: Bologna, Ferrara, Forli, Modena, Parma, Piacenza, Ravenna, Rimini, Reggio Emilia

Le Marche: Pesaro and Urbino, Ancona, Macerata, Ascoli Piceno

Abruzzo and Molise: Giulianova, Pescara, Termoli, Teramo, Gran Sasso, L'Aquila, Molise

Tuscany: Florence, Pisa, Prato, Pistoia, Lucca, Apuan Alps, Serchio Valley, Livorno, Siena, Arezzo, Elba

Umbria: Perugia, Assisi, Via Flaminia, Gualdo Tadino, Spoleto, Valnerina, Todi, Orvieto

Lazio: Viterbo, Three Lakes, Rieti, Tarquinia, Cerveteri, Rome

Campania: Naples, Pozzuolo, Phlegraean Fields, Mount Vesuvius, Pompeii, Sorrento, Amalfi Coast, Paestum, Cilento

Calabria and Basilicata: Maratea, Reggio di Calabria, the Ionian Sea, Basilicata

Puglia: Fóggia (and its Tavoliere), the Gargano Peninsula, Bari, the *Trulli* country, Táranto, the Salentine peninsula, Brindisi, Lecce

Sicily: Palermo, Catania, Siracusa

Sardinia: Cagliari, Olbia, Sassari, Alghero

Characteristics of Italian Cities and Regions

Venice

Venice is perhaps the most dramatic city in Italy. The city of canals and cathedrals has been dubbed "the most romantic city in the world." The primary mode of transportation is by boat or gondola. Imagine a romantic tour at sunset through the Grand Canal past great churches and houses beneath a patchwork of bridges, including the famous Rialto Bridge. The city also features one hundred islands linked by bridges, building facades with gothic windows and Moorish arches, twisting streets, glass chandeliers, and elegant piazzas. One of the islands, Murano, is famous for glass making, while another, Burano, is known for its lace. And, just outside the city is Verona, which was the setting for Shakespeare's *Romeo and Juliet,* and which features the ancient Arena.

Venice is also well known for its annual Carnival held in the spring, in which revelers fill the streets adorned in elaborate costumes and whimsical masks.

There are many ways to transport Venice into your wedding atmosphere. If your wedding site contains a body of water, such as a swimming pool, pond, or lake, you could float a gondola or two in it. Or, if your wedding takes place near the coastline, you and your new spouse could schedule a romantic interlude for two aboard a gondola at sunset, with a bottle of champagne, two glasses, and a gondolier. You might also incorporate touches of Carnival, with masks or pieces of Murano glass as centerpieces.

Tuscany

The region of Tuscany conjures up images of vineyards, wineries, art, and villas under the stars. Tuscany features an alluring countryside, with rolling hillsides, quaint villas, and cottages and castles. Among highlights of Tuscany are pastoral vistas, medieval towns, historical monuments, cypress and olive trees, and vineyards, including the famous Chianti region.

There are museums, such as San Gimignano Museo Civico, with frescoes in the courtyard and works by Pinturicchio, Bartolo di Fredi, Benozzo, Gozzoli, and Filippino Lippi. Also included is the famous early fourteenth-century *Wedding Scene,* a fresco by Memmo di Filippucci, which shows a couple sharing a bath and going to bed. The amazing region of Tuscany has been described as an unspoiled mountainous evergreen miracle.

In addition, this region features the Tuscan Archipelago, a cluster of spread-out islands—Elba, Giglio, Giannuti, Pianosa, Montecristo, and Capraia. Here are monasteries left by monks of the middle ages, Romanesque churches and castles, and remains of Spanish architecture.

Add a touch of Tuscany to your wedding by holding it in a garden setting or at a winery. Decorate the venue in a vineyard motif using grapes and vines. Copies of fourteenth-century paintings add a Tuscan touch, as can medieval décor, cypress and olive trees and branches, and makeshift villas.

Florence

Florence is a city in the region of Tuscany that has many of its own unique characteristics. It is known for its noisy streets with stony facades, amazing cathedrals, and collection of breathtaking art, including world-famous paintings and statues.

Florence is where the Renaissance was born. Masterpieces here include Michelangelo's statues of Bacchus and David, Cellini's statue of Perseus beheading Medusa, and Botticelli's *The Birth of Venus.* Palaces (palazzos) include the Palazzo Vecchio with its famous sculpture garden, Palazzo Rucellai, and Palazzo Pitti. There are fabulous gardens, like the Vittolone, which includes a line of cypress trees.

Bring Florence to your wedding site with replicas of the statue of David or other masterpieces. You can also spruce up the setting with Renaissance décor.

More Tuscan Towns

Siena features hilly streets, Gothic cathedrals, stone palaces, the fan-shaped Piazza del Campo, where the famous Palio horse race takes place twice a year, and the 300-plus-foot Torre del Mangia, which offers breathtaking views of the countryside.

San Gimignano is a tower-filled medieval town with art galleries, shops, restaurants, and a twelfth-century Romanesque church with walls covered in frescoes and a blue vaulted ceiling flecked with golden stars.

Assisi is the town made famous by St. Francis, the protector of small animals.

Pisa, of course, features the classic Italian landmark, the Leaning Tower of Pisa.

Voterra has stunning vistas, statues in white alabaster, and the Museo Etrusco, which includes 600 ornate funeral urns.

Lucca is set inside a ring of Renaissance walls fronted by gates and huge bastions, and is famed for its olive oil.

Arezszo gives us frescoes, stained glass, and Etruscan pottery.

Cortona is a medieval hilltop town best known for its small museums, churches, and wonderful antique shops.

Spoleto is a charming city that puts on a well-known arts festival.

Add touches from any of these Tuscan cities to your wedding scenery by simply replicating some of the things they are famous for. For example, you could include images of St. Francis with small animals, imitations of Pisa's Leaning Tower, as well as stained glass, antiques, and ornate urns.

Umbria

Umbria is very similar to Tuscany. It consists of a wide-open pastoral countryside and high-mountain wilderness. The picturesque region has been dubbed the "green heart of Italy" and is well known for the beauty and profusion of its medieval hill towns, olive harvest, snow-capped mountains, and Romanesque churches. A wedding in the mountains or in an ornate church has a feel of Umbria. So do olives and medieval art.

Le Marche

Le Marche is a rural patchwork of old towns, hill country, and long, sandy beaches. A field of red poppies and olive trees lies in the heart of its countryside. Other highlights of this region include the city of Fano, with its quaint market scenes and the ornate Fontana della Fortuna, the town of San Leo and its dramatic fortress, and the bell tower of the duomo that rises above it. For a Le Marche feel, think woodsy and hilly. Add red poppies, bell towers, and fountains.

Rome

Rome is filled with history and legend. Antique splendors fill this "Eternal City," which is the center of the Christian world and a place where numerous artists and architects once flocked to work. Magnificent architectural masterpieces were created during the Renaissance and Baroque periods, and the legacy can be seen all over the city and in the surrounding areas. Some outstanding features include St. Peter's, with its majestic dome by Michelangelo; the Coliseum, Rome's greatest amphitheater; and San Giovanni Laterno Cathedral of Rome. Also sight-worthy are the Mosaic of the Doves decorated floor of Hadrian's Villa at Tivoli; Hall of the Philosophers; Dying Galatian; St. John the Baptist portrait; Spinario bronze sculture; Esquiline Venus sculpture; Trajan's Column; and the Arch of Constantine.

Rome is home to many attractions, including the Roman Forum with the bell tower of Santa Francesca Romana and the Vestal Virgins; Corinthian Columns of the Temple of Castor and Pollux; and Vatican City and the Sistine Chapel, with its ceiling frescoes by Michelangelo.

For a Roman touch, anything baroque or religious will do, as will bell towers, Michelangelo-inspired artwork, columns and pillars, fountains, lion statues, palatial architecture, arches, angels, and cherubs.

Milan

Milan (in the region of Lombardy) is best known for shopping, fashion, design, art deco, boutique-lined streets, the legendary opera house La Scala, large cathedrals, and da Vinci's *Last Supper*.

To create a feeling of Milan in your wedding setting, add touches of art deco, modern, sleek, and detailed design, and a replica of da Vinci's *Last Supper*.

Naples

Naples features the narrow streets of Quartieri (Spanish Quarter), Museo Archeologico Nazionale, which exhibits treasures of Pompeii, and the Herculaneum and Farnese collections, which contain classical sculpture, including the Blue Vase and Farnese Bull, Spring Fresco, the Palazzo Reale, and the magnificent glass-roofed interior of the Galleria Umberto.

Among the many treasures of Naples are extraordinary ancient churches, like baroque Gesú Nuovo and gothic Santa Chiara, remarkable museums, such as the vast Capodimonte Museum, and Vesuvius, Europe's only active volcano on the horizon. The center of Naples features a grouping of churches, convents, and palaces.

Naples possesses remnants of various influences over the years, including Greek, Roman, Goth, Norman, Spanish, and French. It is an artistic mix, with almost every style found in Italy, especially baroque and neoclassical. Included are Guiseppe Sammartino's sculpture of the *Veiled Christ* in Spaccenapoli's Sanserovo chapel; the grand Palazzo Reale; Piazza Bellini; and the twelfth-century Castel Nuovo, with its Renaissance-style triumphal arch.

Arbors, columns, benches, pizzarias, Roman copies of Greek masterworks, hidden pathways, castles, Baroque palaces, terraced vineyards, medieval buildings, Renaissance architecture, and relics of the Roman era are all features that would add a touch of Naples to your décor.

The Amalfi Coast

The Amalfi Coast (in the region of Campania), along the southwest coast from Sorrento down to Positano, and including Positano, Montepertuso, and Praiano, features classic Mediterranean scenery. The spectacular coastline includes beaches and the islands around the Bay of Naples. The landscape includes a mixture of rocks, forests, and winding roads around towering cliffs overlooking sandy shores and bright blue water. Ravello, a hilltop town along the Amalfi Coast, is known for rustic villas, lush gardens, fascinating cathedrals, and a breathtaking view of the Amalfi coastline.

The Ligurian Coast

Also known as the "Italian Riviera" or "Riviera of Flowers," the Ligurian Coast is a commercially developed strip of coast, bordered by terraced mountain villages where olives and vines are cultivated. This chic coast is famous for its thriving ports and illustrious resorts, which include Alassio, Rapallo, Portofino, Portovenere, and Cinque Terra. The Ligurian Coast features mild climates, steep cliffs, hanging gardens, old fishing towns, and the abundant growth of palms, olives, vines, lemons, oranges, and flowers of the most dazzling colors.

Within the coast is the city of Genoa, Italy's most important commercial port, with its narrow streets, old-town ambience, natural harbor against backdrop of mountains, elevated highway, huge docks, warehouses, alleys, palaces, gardens, and art. It also features the Lanterna lighthouse, built in the twelfth century.

The "Riviera of Flowers" includes the city of San Remo, the flower capital of the coast. This colorful port has the largest flower market in the world. It is also known for its casino. The Ligurian coast's Portofino peninsula is the most exclusive harbor and resort town in Italy, with many yachts and pastel-colored houses near the pebbly beach at Camogli.

If your wedding is held near the ocean, on the beach, in a resort town, or overlooking a body of water, you can add several touches of Italy's coastal cities. Much of what is seen along the Amalfi and Ligurian coasts are products of nature, so a big part of setting the scene would have to do with the location you choose to hold your celebration. However, you can add further touches of the "Riviera of Flowers" by infusing the entire location with brightly colored flowers of every variety. You can also add lighthouses, palm trees, lemons, olives, and oranges.

Pompeii

Pompeii is best known for Santa Maria Capua Vetere, a ruined Roman amphitheater, ornate fountains, such as one in the gardens of the Palazzo Reale at Caserta, an ornate second-century Roman arch in Benevento, and the busy port of Salerno. Incorporate fountains and ornate arches for a slice of Pompeii.

Sicily

Sicily is at the most southern part of Italy. This impressive region is known as the crossroads of Mediterranean civilizations. It features beaches, nature preserves, remote hill towns, and plains highlighted with mountain ranges, which are known for spring flowers, wild life, walnut trees, citrus groves, and vineyards.

Pasta in jars makes a great decorative statement in the Italian kitchen.

A platter of Italian cookies is a typical accompanying dessert to wedding cake at an Italian wedding.

Oil and vinegar in clever grape-cluster decanters makes a nice statement on the wedding celebration table.

Chianti is a popular choice of wine served at an Italian wedding.

An example of a table card for a table named after a city in Italy

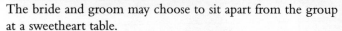

The bride and groom may choose to sit apart from the group at a sweetheart table.

Jordan almonds, also known as "confetti," the quintessential Italian wedding favor

A creative centerpiece, replete with ivy and real grapes

More ideas for packaging wedding favors

Clever grape candle-holders like these can augment the festive setting.

Consider making a framed collage of
your wedding souvenirs as a keepsake.

A gondola makes its way down one of
the many canals of Venice, a wonderful place to honeymoon.

Another view of romantic Venice

Dad's favorite place was italy. He traveled there frequently and embraced the culture wholeheartedly. Here he is seeing the sights while stationed in Europe with the U.S. Army in the 1950s.

Dad in front of a fountain in Rome

My father in Pisa

At the Coliseum

Sicily is known for its wine and its ruins, including the magnificent Valley of the Temples at Agrigento. This is an impressive set of Greek ruins dating back to the fifth century BCE. Sicily is the crossroads of Mediterranean civilizations, and features the influences of many different cultures. Over the last 3,000 years, Sicily has been exposed to new cultures, ideas, and artistic techniques, and as a result, showcases a variety of cities, villages, temples, and impressive works of art. Relics of Romans, Arabs, Normans, the French and Spanish can be found here in the form of temples, theaters, and churches.

A Mediterranean motif on a summer day with lots of colorful spring flowers is a great way to capture Sicily in your wedding scenery. Also, you can add touches of Greece, Spain, and other cultures, as well as ruins, stone sculptures, and vineyard influences.

Palermo

Palermo is the capital city of Sicily and one of Europe's most beautiful cities with its gardens, villas, palaces, and churches in a variety of architectural styles. The city is a mix of Asian and European influence, containing architecture ranging in style from Arabic to Roman baroque and art nouveau, along with Norman art and architecture, baroque churches, and medieval streets and markets.

Sardinia

The island of Sardinia has an interior of rolling grasslands adorned with myrtle, wild thyme, prickly pears, and dwarf oaks bordered by a coastline of translucent sea, isolated coves, and sandy beaches and caves. To add hint of Sardinia to your wedding theme, include baskets or floral arrangements containing myrtle, wild thyme, and prickly pears.

Color Schemes

The color scheme you choose for your wedding is a matter of personal preference, though it may be contingent on the time of year or season, the time of day the wedding is held, and the location. Your color scheme will be woven throughout the wedding—the bridesmaids' dresses and flowers, tablecloths, napkins, floral arrangements, and so on. So while there are no particular colors that make a wedding decidedly Italian, you may want to focus on those colors that flow with the rest of the scene you set and the atmosphere you create.

Italy's national colors are red, white, and green. These may work especially well for the winter or the evening, and certainly around Christmas time. Or, you could create variations of these colors, using maroon, burgundy, or mauve instead of red with white and any shade of green. You're sure to find a color combination that works for any time of the year.

For an outdoor wedding, especially in spring or summer, you might consider soft shades such as pink, blue, lavender, light green, or yellow. Think pale pink or yellow roses with light materials. For a wedding held in fall or winter or in the evening, deeper, darker shades work well. Picture deep red roses with rich black velvet. Your color scheme options are limitless.

Flowers

Deciding on the types of flowers to use in your wedding is as much of a personal choice as your color scheme. And the types of flowers you choose to embellish your wedding scene may coordinate with the bridal bouquets.

While there are favorite wedding flowers—roses, lilies, and the traditional Italian wedding flower, the orange blossom—there are no rules. You may have a favorite type of flower in mind, or the florist you hire can help you decide. Some choose flowers based on what they symbolize (see chapter 6). But for the most part, the flowers you choose in decorating your wedding site are meant to help create the mood you desire.

Floral arrangements are used throughout the wedding, from the ceremony: flowers at the church altar, lining the pews and the aisle, and embellishing an arbor—to the reception: the centerpieces on the dining tables and arrangements in various locations.

For your Italian wedding, choose flowers that complement the rest of the scene as well as your color scheme, the location and its features, the time of year, and so on. Consider how the flowers work together with other decorative aspects at your site, including lighting, candles, plants, and props.

When discussing floral arrangement possibilities with your florist, get an idea of different types of containers they can be displayed in or on—vases, urns, bowls, baskets, pots, and candelabra—as well as greenery accents that can be used—ivy, moss, fern leaves, baby's breath, twigs, and branches. And then there are many alternative arrangement ideas that add to or may even replace traditional floral arrangements. Fruit such as grapes, apples, pears, and oranges add a nice touch to floral arrangements.

Floral Arrangement Samples

Following are some examples of floral arrangements to use at your reception site, either as centerpieces or as decorations on gifts, cake, and banquet tables; in corners, bathrooms, entryways; the garden, and so on.

For a simple, elegant, and summery look use wide, shallow glass containers, such as a punch bowl or salad bowl, and fill them with five or so huge white flowers with strong petals and leaves, such as Casablanca lilies or peonies. Or, in a tumbler-style vase or ice bucket, display tall French lilacs or hydrangeas.

For springy pinks and purples, arrange the following combinations in vases of your choice: deep purple—violet hydrangea with green kale leaves; pinks and purples—pink garden roses, purple lilacs, lavender spray roses, and hydrangea—or pale pink tulips with long leaves and grape-hyacinth blooms; pink and white—pink and white peonies with lavender sweet peas and white lilacs; a mixed bouquet of garden roses, sweet peas, geraniums, and lavender lisianthus.

A Mediterranean arrangement includes green grapes, peonies, dahlias, and ivy; or a mixture of garden roses, green grapes, and ivy.

For a traditional Italian centerpieces, put branches of fragrant orange blossoms in any kind of vase or bowl.

Tall potted floral arrangements can be made with flowers with long, sturdy stems, such as sunflowers, gerberas, mixed roses, brodiaea, and bouvardia, and placed in terra-cotta pots and florist's foam. The stems are tied together with ribbon and stand tall in the pot.

Centerpieces

While there are thousands of ways to use flowers in centerpieces, there are also many non-floral and combination floral/non-floral ideas as well. These include candles, herbs, plants, branches, water, rocks, fruit and other food items, collections of objects, and whimsical displays. Get creative with your centerpieces. Go with the traditional flower arrangements with an Italian touch, a mixture of candles and flowers, or something completely unusual. You or a friend or relative can make your own arrangements, or you can have them done by a florist or other professional or even buy them already made. Following are some innovative ideas for centerpieces for your Italian wedding.

Flower Boat. A large long, narrow, boat-like platter serves as the base. Finished, it resembles a gondola. Fill with greenery and assorted flowers and place in the middle of a long oval or rectangular table, with table runners used instead of a tablecloth.

Herb Centerpiece. Using three variegated stacked terra-cotta pots, floral foam, and individual sprigs of parsley, sage, and rosemary (which are used in many Italian recipes), arrange the herbs to cascade down from the pots, creating a very Tuscan look. Or, arrange purple basil, mint, sage, and rosemary in a simple vase.

Water Centerpiece. Using terra-cotta pots and smooth stones or river rocks, water, and a single flower, such as a garden rose, you can make a tropical-looking centerpiece quickly and easily. This goes well with a Mediterranean, Venetian, or Coastal Italy theme.

Floating Candle Centerpiece. Fill a clear glass bowl with water, add a lilac branch and float three candles on the water.

Artful Centerpiece. Have an artist create an Italian-style painting on a small canvas for each table. Prop each painting on a miniature easel, surrounded with votive candles in small glass holders, and sprinkle rose petals around it. You can also wrap vines of miniature ivy around the legs of the easel.

Food Centerpiece. Set up individual picnic trays on each table, consisting of a wooden tray with a red-and-white gingham cloth, bottle of Chianti, bunches of grapes, block of cheese, tear bread, salami, and a knife.

Italian Fruit Basket. You can find a wide selection of baskets in various sizes and materials, such as a natural bird's nest basket. Line the bottom with styrofoam and fill with an assortment of real or artificial fruit of all types—grapes, pears, apples, oranges, bananas, and pineapples—and coordinated with silk flowers. Wrap ivy and moss around the handle. You can also use oranges, lemons, and limes or vegetables like artichokes, corn on the cob, carrots, and radishes.

Italian Wedding Traditional Centerpiece. For fun, why not incorporate Italian wedding traditions into your centerpieces with a different tradition for each table. This will encourage guests to get up and mingle to find out what's on the other tables. On one table, you could feature an art deco clear vase filled with broken glass and have a card propped up next to it explaining the glass-breaking tradition. Others might be of fake white doves in a decorative birdcage, a bride doll with a torn veil, pieces of iron arranged in a unique design, a cut up tie, white purse, tarantula, a tiered display of Jordan almonds, large satin bows, and a statue of Juno, the Roman goddess of marriage.

More Centerpiece Ideas. Here are a few more ideas you might try: Grapevine wreaths; tapers placed in a wreath of baby's breath and greenery; little trees with white lights; mini villas (made from birdhouses or doll houses, or handmade replicas); flowers in unusual containers such as wooden crates or hollowed-out fruit; miniature gondolas with flowers, candles, candies, or food inside; bowls of water with mini gondolas floating in them along with floating flowers and candles; tiered Italian pastries; ice sculptures; baskets of fruit; Italian candy or bread; topiaries of Italian landmarks, such as the Leaning Tower; bell towers or duomos; statues; miniature arbors; jars of dried pasta, garlic, and olives; unique bottles filled with olive oil and herbs; wine bottles serving as candle holders; and an ivy arch or rose tree.

Arbors

Arbors, or garden arches, are very elegant and romantic. If a wedding ceremony is held outside, an arbor makes a great altar. It can also be used throughout the reception site—over doorways, entrances, or pathways, over the wedding cake, sweethearts' table, or sitting areas (inside or out). The arched shape is often seen in Italian architecture, making arbors great enhancements for Italian weddings. They come in many styles and materials—wood, lattice, wire, plastic, brass, or iron—and can be rented or bought. Arbors can be subtly or elaborately decorated with tulle, flowers, greenery, ribbon, white lights, grapes, ivy, balloons—you name it.

For a full floral effect, completely cover a wire or iron arch with mixed spring flowers and leaves. This is great for a springtime or summer wedding in a garden with lots of greenery and wildflowers. For a soft, light, and romantic touch, adorn a white lattice arbor with cascading tulle and bunches of soft-colored roses and greenery. For a rustic, woodsy look, create your own arbor out of branches and wrap slightly with bougainvillea, ivy, or vines.

Tents

Using a tent adds protection from heat and rain for an outdoor wedding and makes a great blank canvas for decorating, allowing you to do just about anything to your setting. Tents can be found at many rental companies in a variety of sizes and styles. Try one large tent, a few medium-sized, or a number of small ones, with or without sides, floors, and different lighting possibilities.

Umbrellas

If the wedding reception, or part of it, is to be held outdoors, you might consider putting up large umbrellas, either freestanding or attached to tables. These umbrellas, which come in many styles, colors, and materials, can be purchased from furniture, hardware, or home and garden stores, as well as from some drug stores, and even rented. Not only do umbrellas provide shelter from the sun, they add an elegant Italian café touch.

Trees

For an outdoor wedding, consider an outdoor location with lots of trees. Not only do they provide shade and beauty, immense tree growth is representative of much of the land in Italy. Throughout the country, there are trees of almost every kind, and various regions specialize in certain varieties.

While the wedding location may or may not have many trees and plant life, you can bring in potted trees and plants of almost any kind. In fact, potted varieties are a great addition to even a heavily vegetative site. Garden centers carry a wide variety of trees, plants, and pots that will work well with your scenery. And these aren't just for outside, you can bring nature indoors as well. Also look for silk trees and plants to enhance your wedding décor.

Lighting

When it comes to a setting, lighting is a very important consideration. If your reception is being held indoors, the location most likely has its own lighting, via ceiling fixtures, chandeliers, and lamps, which may or may not be able to be dimmed. Outdoors, you might be relying on natural light. However, you can enhance the lighting in many situations, especially after dark.

For garden radiance, add white twinkle lights to as many spots as possible—trees and bushes, along fences and gates are just a couple of places. There is nothing more fantastic than thousands of white lights glittering in the night. You can also string lengths of tiny white lights along gauzy fabric and hang the material from ceilings, windows, doorways, or anywhere else you choose. Also, string lights in potted trees and plants, and on the inside of tents, umbrellas, and patios.

Light up your garden further with luminary bags along walkways. You can find white luminary bags, lined with fire resistant wax, at many craft and specialty stores and in wedding supply catalogs. Anchor the bags with sand or gravel and place votive candles inside.

An easy, dramatic, and popular way to enhance lighting is with candles, which can be used in centerpieces and just about anywhere. Candle sizes and varieties are endless—tapers, votives, tea lights, floating, and pillars are just a few. There are many choices when it comes to displaying candles, with different types of candle holders, candelabra, sconces, jars, and bowls. And then there are lanterns, garden torches, sparklers, miniature lamps, and spotlights.

Table Settings

How you arrange the dining tables at your wedding will vary, depending on the number of guests, location, and so on. Choices will include the size and shape of the tables—round, oval, square, or rectangular, in varying sizes—as well as chairs, tablecloths and napkins, and all the accoutrements of a properly set table. Your color scheme and centerpieces will also play a role in your table settings.

In many cases the caterer will set the tables to your preference. You might have a certain way you like the napkins folded or the glasses and silverware arranged that you can share with your caterer ahead of time. Include wedding favors, thank you notes, and menu cards at the place settings. You can assign seating, or let guests sit where they choose.

You may seat the bridal party together at one table—often a long table at the front of the room facing the guests—or simply have a sweetheart table for bride and groom, and allow the bridal party to sit with their families and loved ones. Or, you and your spouse can share a table with your parents.

Sweetheart Tables

It is very romantic to have a small intimate table set up for the bride and groom. This table can be adorned like the guest tables or be completely different with unique flowers, centerpiece, and other adornments. It might also feature an ice bucket with champagne and special toasting flutes.

The sweetheart table can be placed at the front or middle of the room, on a stage or riser, under a tree or arbor, or in a secluded corner.

Design Terms

When creating an Italian ambience, and studying the various art, architecture, and decorating styles of Italy, there are a few terms that describe certain aspects of design that you'll want to become familiar with. Following is a sampling of design terms.

Renaissance. The period between 1400 and 1600, which was considered a "rebirth" and comprised of two principal components: a revival of the classical forms developed by the ancient Greeks and Romans; and a renewed vitality and spirit highlighting the qualities of humanity. The Renaissance style of building and decoration succeeded Gothic and aimed to reproduce the forms of classical ornamentation.

Baroque. A style of architecture that involves an elaborate and ornate design. The baroque décor is that of simple function represented in ornamental design, with lots of irregularly-shaped features and eccentric style.

Gothic. An architectural style characterized by pointed arches as the main feature.

Medieval. Pertaining to the Middle Ages, the period between about the eighth and mid-fifteenth centuries.

Romanesque. A style of architecture and design characterized by round arches and vaults and extensive ornaments.

Italian Wedding Scenes

This section features ideas on how to conjure up a sensual Italian experience for your Italian wedding. Whether a charming garden setting, a coastal paradise, or a regal Roman empire is your idea of the perfect wedding setting, there's something in this section for you.

A Lush Italian Garden

An Italian wedding outdoors can be breathtaking. You can create a scene resembling an Italian fantasyland in the midst of fresh air and greenery, lit by the afternoon sun, a sunset, or starlight. A florist or a talented friend can design a Mediterranean motif throughout the garden or yard using natural decorative items, such as fresh red, purple, or green grapes, pliable vines, leafy ivy, and pastel and white garden roses. For an added effect, scatter rose petals here and there—on banquet and guest tables and throughout the garden.

If you hold the ceremony outdoors, set up guests' chairs amid shady trees. White wood fold-up chairs work well in this setting. Drape white tulle from the chairs along the "aisle" and secure with satin ribbon that coordinates with your color scheme. Note that soft pinks work well, especially in spring and summer. For the altar, a self-standing white iron arbor can be decorated with vines and ivy intertwined and clusters of grapes and roses hanging from it. These clusters appear to grow from the arbor, giving it a vineyard feeling. The aisle leading up to the altar can be sparsely or heavily sprinkled with pale pink rose petals.

Find a separate area to set up dinner seating. Round tables for ten, draped with floor-length white tablecloths, can be set up on flat grass or on a cement patio or driveway. Tall white canvas umbrellas can be set up in between the tables. Not only do they provide shade to your guests if the wedding reception takes place during the day, they also add to the garden look and help pull everything together.

For an elegant touch, especially if the wedding takes place at twilight, guest table centerpieces might feature ornate silver and crystal hurricane lamps enhanced with grapes and roses tied on with ivy and a ribbon. At night, the lighted candles create a romantic glow throughout the garden.

As a focal point of the dinner area, set up a separate romantic sweetheart table for the bride and groom. This table can be propped on a riser overlooking the guest tables, allowing the wedding couple to be the king and queen of the day. It can be set with a white tablecloth and china place settings, silverware, and crystal from the couple's own gift registry. The table looks elegant with vines and moss draped across the front with ivy and roses interspersed. If location permits, place the table under a tree. For a dramatic effect, hang a natural-looking garden chandelier from the branches above. The chandelier can be crafted out of a round or donut-shaped styrofoam, covered with moss, grapes, roses, and three or four candles. When the sun goes down, light the candles and your chandelier illuminates the table.

Tuscan Countryside

Hold the wedding outdoors in a large grassy area with lots of hills and trees. This could perhaps be at a resort or country club, in a vacant field, or on a large lawn. Construct wood huts, villas, or tents. Hold the wedding ceremony in a gazebo draped with moss, vines, ivy, and bunches of deep purple grapes hanging from vines that are wrapped around the gazebo posts. Rent or purchase ornate wood and iron benches, or make logs into seats for guests to sit on during the ceremony.

Utilize the natural setting. Hold the ceremony at twilight. Build a shrine to the Virgin Mary into a tree stump. Re-create a charming castle with rotundas and multitiered towers, tucked into a hillside that is speckled with yellow and purple wildflowers.

In a wide open space you can spread out, using different locations for various aspects of the celebration, while utilizing nature: lots of twigs and branches, draped with natural materials. Go heavy on the "vineyard" look, wrapping grapevines and dangling bunches of grapes everywhere. The look can be rustic/chic. For dining tables, use leveled-off tree stumps or cement made to look like tree stumps, topped with clear glass. Surround them with folding chairs with chair covers.

For centerpieces, gather rustic vases from garage sales, antique shops, or craft stores (and paint if necessary), and fill them with varied-length twigs, wrapped and draped with twine, and vines with grapes hanging from them. A combination of green and red or purple grapes looks gorgeous. Accent with dark green moss, ferns, and baby's breath. Scatter small tables and chairs in remote sitting areas under "vineyard arches," or arbors adorned in grapes and vines.

Mediterranean Paradise

The Mediterranean areas of Italy feature water and a tropical feeling, which you can re-create in your setting. Bring in many forms of water—fountains, waterfalls, pools, ponds, and birdbaths. An aquarium with colorful tropical fish adds a nice touch. Inquire if nearby pet stores offer or can recommend a rental service to provide aquarium setups. Infuse the setting with unique ornate fountains of various sizes and textures—cement, wood, and marble—and saturate the air with the soothing sounds of running water. You can find fountains everywhere, from garden shops to hardware stores.

Decorate the setting with large potted trees and plants and hanging plants in oversized ornate pots. Other touches can include gardenias, baskets of fruit, large crystal punch bowls filled with tropical drinks, and white twinkle lights in the potted trees at night. The Mediterranean touch is great for summer weddings near the beach or a lake and for affairs serving a seafood menu.

Roman Empire

For a Romanesque ambience, think pillars, columns, domes, and arches. To decorate your wedding scene you will want to take advantage of bold shapes and textures. The Roman style includes Renaissance, Baroque, and Gothic touches. Re-create an ancient and artistic flavor buy using textured columns from arts and crafts stores, either finished or unfinished. Use them in abundance—to prop plants and floral arrangements, and top with glass to use as tables. Decorate your interior with ancient looking artwork in heavy ornate frames—preferably gold or dark wood. Incorporate intricate statues—reproductions of famous works, as well as cherubs, angels, and lions.

Re-create well-known Roman landmarks, such as the Coliseum. You might hold your reception in a stadium, arena, or amphitheater, and decorate with *Gladiator* props, including armor, shields, swords, and animal statues.

For a dramatic Romanesque sweetheart table, create a semicircle out of tall columns as a backdrop for an ornate table for two. Buy or rent three or four six-foot-tall white columns as well as two or three shorter ones and arrange them in a semicircle. Top each column with an ornate pot, urn, or vase filled with cascading white flowers and lush greenery. Dramatically drape tulle from the columns. Set up the table inside this regal arc. Use a small table for two, and two chairs covered in flowing seat covers. Cover the table in an elaborate satin, silk, or taffeta two-tiered ruffled white, gold, or bronze tablecloth and drape floral garlands from it.

Napoli Café Terrace

Reconstruct a scene from the streets of Naples, such as a café on Piazza Trieste e Trento. The scene is drawn from a gray stone brick streetscape, lined with laundry-festooned balconies, flower-enhanced shrines, and clusters of parked motor scooters. Quaint outdoor cafés covered with terraces and speckled with little tables and abundant plants and flowers are the focal point. To re-create this scene, simulate a grand terrace, using a tent, tarp, or other material upon rope attached to wooden poles. Set up several small tables and chairs under the terrace and surround the entire area with wrought-iron fencing, statuesque street lamps, and large terra-cotta pots of flowers, such as red gardenias. Also fill huge wooden planters with varied greenery.

To imitate the surrounding scenery, drape colorful material or scarves on walls, balconies, and shelves and line up several motor scooters. For added effect, top each table with red-and-white checked tablecloths, and set up trays of breads and pastries.

Making Your Own Decorations

You, a helpful and creative friend, or a hired artist can make some wonderful Italian decorations with very little effort. Many of these can be used again later. Several arts and crafts stores carry a selection of supplies and materials to create these items.

Make silk floral spring bushes arranged in terra-cotta pots or large baskets. You can find great, natural-looking silk trees in many varieties—ficus, palm, or fern. Place them in ornate pottery, enhance them with white lights, and scatter them throughout your setting.

Make vineyard decorations using garlands, fake grapes, swags, bushes, wreaths, ivy leaves, and wire. Use a wire wreath, six large bunches of artificial grapes, and a long strand of wired silk ivy and wire. Place the grapes around the wreath and secure them with wire. Wrap ivy around the wreath and arrange the leaves. You can also buy shepherd's hooks, garden arches, and decorative trellises to adorn with the same types of garnishes. Other touches might include wind chimes, patio torches, and glass gazing balls.

12

Unique Italian Touches

IN ADDITION TO THE meaningful traditions, the festive practices, the abundant food and drink, and the beautiful visual enhancements that make Italian weddings so special, you might want to add a few unique touches for effect. Some of these are extensions of elements we're already discussed, while others are entirely new, and intended for all phases of your wedding-planning process.

Welcome to Italia

Instead of using numbers to designate seating assignment, name your tables after cities in Italy—Rome, Milan, Naples, Venice, and so on. You can also name them after Italian artists, musicians, celebrities, wines, foods, or landmarks. Have someone use calligraphy to write the names of the tables on cards, or use a computer in a cursive font style to create the look of calligraphy. Once the table names are printed on the cards, paint, stencil, or hire an artist to paint grapes and vines, flowers, or other images on them. You can also draw or paint a picture symbolizing that particular city or region. For example, on the card for the Venice table, include an illustration of a gondola; for the Rome table, a portrait of the Pope; and for the Turin table, a picture of a Fiat (that's where the Fiat plant is located).

Place the cards on table cardholders, which can be rented from a party rental company or borrowed from your florist or caterer. Set up guest seating assignments, or "destination" cards somewhere near the entrance so guests will see and pick them up as they arrive. Once guests find their names and pick up their seating cards, they can find their tables' names on the large cards enhanced with lovely painted images.

Most seating assignment cards are printed on business-card size cardboard folded over so they are easy to display and don't take up too much space. These cards often feature the guests' names and underneath, the table number or name. You can get creative with these cards, using any shape, size or object, that you please.

For a whimsical approach, let guests pick up miniature maps of Italy, with their names, their table's name, and an "x" marking that city on the map. Print the guests' names and table names on their proper places on the map. For example, Milan would be printed near the top, Perugia in the middle, and Catanzaro at the bottom of the boot. Palermo (on the island of Sicily) and Arbatax (on the island of Sardinia) would be on separate and smaller cutouts.

Or, create seating assignment cards that coordinate with the name of the table they are assigned to. For example, for all the guests assigned to the Pisa table, print their names on Leaning Tower of Pisa cutouts; for those at the Montalcino table, wine barrels; for the Milan table, miniature Giorgio Armani shopping bags, and so on.

In addition to naming the tables after cities, name other locations and items, such as banquet, gift, and cocktail tables, bathrooms, the bar, stairways, gardens, and resting areas after Italian landmarks and buildings. Name a staircase "The Spanish Steps"; call the church, chapel, or altar "The Sistine Chapel"; the bar, "Chianti Region," and so on.

Incorporating Italian Artwork
Into Your Wedding Site

Being that Italy is so rich with art, why not infuse your wedding site with some of this artistic richness? There are many ways to add touches of Italian art to your celebration. Prior to the wedding, you and your spouse-to-be could have a portrait done—photographed or painted—in a da Vinci-esque style and display the portrait at your wedding site.

If you have an artistic friend or know an art student (check with a nearby college or art school or high school) you could hire them to do paintings or sculptures, replicating some of the Italian masterpieces. Have them paint the inside of a cloth/tarp/blanket in colorful images of the Sistine Chapel ceiling and drape it over a chosen spot, such as a sitting area, in a bathroom or hallway, or inside a tent used for dining or dancing. Or you might buy, rent, or borrow reproductions of Italian works of art to display throughout your setting. Hang paintings on walls and place statues in gardens, on tables, and on pedestals in corners. You could also use scenic photographs, posters, or paintings of Italy and its scenery.

Have an artist paint frescoes or scenery on wooden planks to put up along walls or be propped up outside as backdrops for sitting areas. Or, have him stencil white sheets or other material with depictions of grapes and vines, Italian architecture, art-works, sculptures, landmarks, café scenes, and more to hang on the walls.

Sculptures can be made out of clay, papier mâché, wood, or stone as well as balloons, topiaries, and blocks of ice. Balloon sculptures can be created by twisting tiny balloons into bunches of grapes, a gondola, or what have you. In addition to displaying balloon sculptures at the wedding site, you can use them as direction markers, along with signs pointing toward the wedding location.

Topiary sculptures can be made with wire as the base, and covered with various greenery, ivy, plants, and flowers. You can also create light sculptures with topiary wire wrapped with white light strands and thin greenery/garland in shapes of Italian landmarks, architecture, and statues, and place them in the garden in the evening.

Ice sculptures can be shaped into various images and add an elegant touch to food, drink, and dessert tables. In addition to having ice carved into Italian sculptures and landmarks, you could have bunches of grapes and other fruit frozen inside big blocks of ice, hollowed out in the middle to hold champagne and white wine bottles. For more frozen effects, freeze individual grapes into ice cubes and serve with various drinks.

Italian Wedding Props

This section points out some fun props that will truly infuse your wedding with an Italian flair.

Gondolas

Gondolas, either life-sized or miniatures can be placed in a pool and anchored with weights. For added elegance, fill them with floral arrangements. Gondolas can also be suspended from the ceiling or a tree, or placed on the ground, tables, pedestals, or risers. They can be made from plywood, styrofoam, clay, or papier mâché and painted the color of your choice.

If you do include actual-size gondolas, in the pool or elsewhere, you could hire a gondolier to offer guests rides. Perhaps a gondola on wheels can be pulled down the street. Hire a musician/singer, dressed in gondolier attire—red and white striped shirt, black pants, and brimmed hat—to serenade guests.

Fountains

Water fountains are very elegant and romantic, and can add an Italian touch to your wedding, as Italy is known for its many beautiful fountains. Fountains can be found in hundreds of styles and sizes at hardware and home and garden stores. You can find fountains to blend in with your scenery indoors or outdoors, ranging from simple to highly ornate with tiers and statues. You can also find miniature water fountains for indoors, on tables and countertops and even to use as centerpieces. There are also special fountains that can be used in a swimming pool, which sit in the middle of the pool and spout to different heights, depending on your preference.

Piazzas, Palazzos, Villas, and Cafés

Create different versions of these common Italian sites and incorporate them into your wedding scheme. Set up mock cafés from which guests are served food and beverages. Create a mock Italian villa, inside which you and your new spouse will sit.

Miniature models of these structures can be made from birdhouses and doll houses, and can feature signs in the front with such names as Palazzo Malatesta, Piazza della Spagna, or Villa Rotonda, or from scratch with wood and other materials. They can also display flowers and other adornments. Other props include various sized Italian flags, fireworks displays, birdbaths, ponds, and fire pits.

It's the Little Things

There are many little details you can add to that make your wedding even more memorable. This section will take you through some of them.

Special hand-towels in the bathrooms. Include hand-towels that have the bride and groom's monogram on them, or Italian phrases, words, or pictures. These can all be done by embroidery shops. Look in the yellow pages for a shop near you.

Purple fluorite vases. The ancient Romans, who admired purple vases carved from fluorite, considered them valuable treasures. You can include fluorite vases, which come in deep purple, deep blue, green, aqua, or clear, or make your own version of these fluorite vases using clear glass painted these colors.

Tiered decorations. Stack three-tiered trays and adorn them with green apples, pears, and grapes as well as hollowed-out apples and pears which hold mini floral arrangements or tea light candles.

Colorful glass. Group martini glasses, the bottoms filled with clear or colored glass marbles and votive candles. Display these on tables, bar tops, fireplace mantels, and so on.

Stacked boxes. For serving and display tables, stack rustic wooden boxes on top of each other, and either paint them or leave them plain for rustic a look.

Italian Heritage Displays

Bring your Italian family into the décor by using these ideas.

Family Trees

Create a family tree, perhaps tracing your ancestors' roots back to Italy, and collect old photos, frame them, and hang them from the tree branches. Display the tree at the wedding on a table in a hallway. Use a manzanita tree with a base or a branch formation of your choice. You might also adorn the tree with flowers, grapes, vines, and ivy.

Ancestor Photo Gallery

Gather old ancestor photos, as well as recent family photos, frame them in ornate frames, and hang them on a wall at the reception or display them on tables. Photos can also be hung on fences, gates, and trees, and placed on dining tables as centerpieces.

Another approach is to create a wall display of ancestors on a large bulletin board, or slab of foam or cardboard covered with fabric. Make copies of original photos and attach them to the board, adding trim with cording.

If you, the bridal couple, have been on a trip to Italy together or separately with your families, place those photos around the site or include them in a video montage. Many videographers will offer a video montage option, in which photos of the bride, groom, their friends, and families are sorted and presented to background music at the beginning of the wedding video.

Drinks Trays

Using large picture frames, create a collage of photos of Italy, or family photos. Screw in drawer handles at both ends and you have a personalized drink and appetizer servers.

Fun Mementos With Art

Here are some fun ways to get your guests involved in the action.

Photo Booth

Have a photo booth set up with Italian scenery backgrounds in which guests can have their pictures taken. Hire or appoint someone to take the picture with a polaroid camera and slip the photo into a decorated photo card/frame, and let guests keep the photo as a memento of the day. Or take the photos with a regular camera and send your guests their pictures with thank you cards.

Caricatures

Hire a cartoonist, maybe a college art student, to do Italian-esque caricatures of guests as mementos.

More Special Guests

There can be more to the entertainment at your Italian wedding than just music and dancing. Here are some other people you can hire to keep your guests happy and well entertained.

Entertainers

Hire various roving Italian musicians and performers to entertain guests throughout the celebration. These might include an accordion player, opera singer, or crooner, such as a Frank Sinatra impersonator. Or you could include impersonators of the Pope and Italian actors and celebrities.

The Godfather

Hire a Godfather impersonator to make an appearance and present the wedding couple with a gift "they can't refuse." Have the band or DJ stop the show announcing a "special guest" and play the theme music to *The Godfather*. Hire a professional actor/impersonator or have a talented and outgoing friend or friend of a friend dress up in a black suit, fedora, and dark sunglasses to play the part.

Prepare a script for him to read with a thick Italian accent. The Godfather can offer the newlyweds an envelope filled with money. This is a whimsical and light-hearted activity that is fun for the guests later in the evening when the mood is even more festive.

Wedding Favor Ideas

While Jordan almond bunches, also called confetti, are traditional Italian wedding favors, there are many ideas for Italian-esque favors to use instead or in addition to them. Favors can also be given at bridal showers, engagement parties, and rehearsal dinners. Following are a few suggestions.

- ❦ Napkin rings that look like small bunches of grapes, found at wineries and gift shops.

- ❦ Tiny bottles of olive oil, which you can make with little antique bottles that you fill with olive oil and herbs, and cork with miniature corks.

- Italian spices in small bags or wrapped in cellophane and placed in little boxes, wrapped with ribbon, or layered in a jar. Spices might include basil, garlic, oregano, and others. A little note with a family recipe that calls on the spices adds a personal touch.

- Sets of four coasters, hand-painted with Italian scenes.

- Miniature Leaning Tower or David statues made of clay, wood, chocolate, or other materials.

- Small white purses filled with candies, such as candy coins, for the women.

- Embroidered handkerchiefs with images of grapes, name of Italian city, map of Italy, or gondolas, for the men.

- Snow globes with Italian scenes inside.

- Potpourri made from Italian flowers, specifically orange blossoms, roses, and lilies, wrapped in tulle and tied with ribbon with a little charm attached of a goddess or a gem.

- Italian cookies, candy, or biscotti, made from a family recipe and wrapped and tied with a bow with a recipe attached.

- Small boxes of candy hearts tied with ribbons and with silk flowers glued on top.

- Miniature bottles of wine.

- Little baskets with herbs, flowers, or candies.

Gifts for Out-of-Town Guests

When out-of-town guests travel to join in your special day, it is customary to leave or send them a "thanks for coming" gift to their hotel room or guest quarters.

For your out-of-town guests, you might create gift boxes filled with information on wedding itineraries, and local sites and restaurants, specifically Italian restaurants, as well as Italian munchies, such as wines, cheeses, salami, bread sticks, mixed fruit, Italian cookies, and candies.

Italiano: The Language of Love

For a sentimental touch, include some Italian language in your wedding celebration. You could include some Italian words or phrases in your wedding vows, which can be translated in the wedding program. Have the inside of your husband-to-be's wedding ring engraved with an Italian phrase, such as "Ti amo per la vita," which is Italian for "I love you for life," followed by your wedding date. Surprise him with this message during a quiet moment alone after the ceremony. Ask him to remove the ring and look inside at the inscription.

You can go all out and hire a plane with a banner, a blimp, or sky writer to fly overhead at a certain time with an Italian expression. Or, take out a personal ad in the newspaper with an Italian love message for him, and plan a way for him to come across it.

A Few "Words" About Italian Wedding Traditions

Wedding programs are a great way to involve guests in your wedding celebration. There are lots of ways to create programs, from a simple one-sheet version that includes the names of the bridal party to an elaborate booklet with everything from how the bridal couple met to where they are going on their honeymoon.

Some great information to include in your program are explanations of important parts of your wedding ceremony and celebration, the Italian customs and their meanings, titles of songs and readings, brief introductions to all the key players, and acknowledgments. Put a photo of you and your beloved on the front cover.

Invitations, Save-the-Date, and Engagement Announcements

Add an Italian touch to invitations and other cards you mail to your guests during the wedding process. For an invitation, make Romanesque scrolls on parchment paper, wrapped in acanthus leaves, or in a trumpet, or secured with grape bunch napkin rings. You can also use this technique with your wedding programs or menus at the wedding.

To announce your engagement and wedding date, write the message on Italian flags, or on a separate card with an Italian flag attached. Cut out a map of Italy and place the message inside. Make a card with a drawing or painting of a diamond engagement ring and include some wording about the ancient Romans' beliefs and use of diamond engagement rings (see chapter 4). On the card, you could glue on a large rhinestone as the stone in the ring. Inside the card, include the information about the engagement or wedding. Or simply write your message on a white panel card embossed with grapes or other Italian-esque designs.

Birds of a Feather

While the tradition of releasing white doves is practiced at some Italian weddings, another idea is to incorporate birds into the overall setting. Find an ornate birdcage (or cages), and decorate with flowers, tulle, and ribbon in the motif of your wedding, for a pair of white doves or peach-faced lovebirds. There are companies that rent out doves for release and display. Check with them or a local pet store to see if they'll lend lovebirds as well.

Consider purchasing a pair of lovebirds to keep after the wedding. Name the bird couple after Italian relatives or celebrities, such as Sophia and Marcello. Designate their cage a bird villa named after an Italian landmark. You might also consider finches in bamboo cages or trained parrots on perches for a Mediterranean wedding.

Lucky Charms

Find or have custom-made a charm of Juno, goddess of marriage, or Fortuna. You could include drawings or paintings of these good luck symbols with your other art displays or in the bathrooms or resting areas.

Although the "something old, something new, something borrowed, something blue" adage is not Italian, you could incorporate it with an Italian flair. In your wedding, you can have all "old" traditions, passed down from the ages; "new" can represent your new life together as a married couple, as well as your wedding because it's your own; "borrowed" could be to use a custom you like from another culture; and "blue" could be the sky, water, or an Italian blue glass goblet or vase.

This theme can be incorporated into a food table with an old recipe passed down from the generations, a new recipe, a borrowed recipe from a friend, cookbook or restaurant, and a food with a blue ingredient in it, such as blueberry pie.

Transportation

While most couples these days are taken to and from the wedding in a rented limousine, there are many other forms of transportation from which to choose. For an Italian touch, you might consider being chauffeured in a mock gondola, which can be a float either motor powered or pulled by foot, bike, or horse.

Consider having a Roman chariot drawn by horse take you away, or hop onto an armored horse. You could rent an Italian automobile, such as a Ferrari or Fiat, or drive off on a Vespa motor scooter.

Ideas During Planning

Add some fun, relaxation, education, and exploration of your culture to your wedding planning experience. During the busy wedding planning process, schedule some time, every week or every two weeks or so to do something special for yourself, your groom-to-be, or family. And add Italian flavor to these activities. Some of these activities will get you in touch with your Italian roots, while others will give you quality time with the ones you love.

One idea might be to rent and watch Italian movies, or movies with Italian settings or characters, such as *Moonstruck, Saturday Night Fever, The Godfather, Cinema Paradiso, The Monster, La Dolce Vita, Il Postino, The Bicycle Thief, The Garden of the Finzi-Continis, La Strada,* or *Roman Holiday.* Or plan a romantic date for you and your fiancé at an elegant Italian restaurant, maybe one you have never tried.

For family and friends, plan and cook a big Italian meal for a large group. Play Italian music in the background and set your table with Italian touches, as discussed in chapter 11. Buy a new Italian cookbook and sample a recipe. Spend a day with your mom, grandma, an aunt, or other Italian relative or family friend who is a great cook and have her (or him) teach you how to make those wonderful meatballs, manicotti, sauce, or pastries.

Or, get in touch with an older Italian relative either in person or via phone, and spend time conversing with him, learning more about your family heritage, what life was like back in the old days in Italy, all while giving an older relative some much-appreciated company.

You might also get in touch with the arts. Attend an opera, visit a museum, draw or paint something, take an art class, spend some time in the library viewing books on Italian art. Or, take an Italian language or cooking class.

Bridal Shower Ideas

There are numerous ways to incorporate an Italian theme into bridal showers, with the food, music, décor, games, and activities. Here are just a few ideas.

Name That Italian Celebrity

As an ice-breaker activity, fill out name cards with different famous Italian actors, models, artists, authors, scientists, composers, singers, explorers, athletes, politicians, and so on. As each guest enters the shower, place a name card on her back, without her seeing the name on the card. Guests can look at each other's name tags, asking each other yes or no questions about the names on their backs. If a person guesses the correct name, she can remove the name tag. This way, people are encouraged to mingle until everyone has guessed the correct name.

Another activity using famous Italians could be a simple shower game where everyone has to write down as many names as they can think of within a certain amount of time. The person who writes the most names wins a prize.

Name That Italian Recipe

Another game to play at an Italian bridal shower is a food tasting game, in which guests taste different Italian foods—appetizers, pasta dishes, desserts—and write down as many ingredients as they think they can taste in the foods. They can also make up their own recipe for the dish. The one who comes closest to the real recipe wins.

Another twist on this contest could be to have everyone bring a printout of their favorite Italian recipe and then put it into a notebook/Italian cookbook. For those who choose to participate, hold a cooking competition, in which guests prepare an Italian dish, which everyone tastes and then decides on a winner.

Pin the City on the Map

Using large cutout cardboard shapes of Italy and small stickers or cardboard puzzle pieces with different Italian cities, have guests split up into three or four groups and put the Italian cities in their proper places on the map. The group that comes the closest to being accurate wins.

Translate the Italian Phrases

Compile about ten or so Italian phrases that have to do with love or marriage, and have guests translate them to the best of their ability. Whoever gets the most that are the closest to being correct wins.

Italian Mad Libs

As in the traditional game, the hostess or maid of honor could ask the bride for a series of words and then write down the answers. Those answers are then used to fill in the blanks of a silly story in an Italian setting and read aloud to the guests.

Baking Italian Cookies

As a shower activity, everyone can take part in preparing pre-selected recipes for Italian cookies, leave them to bake while guests are participating in other activities. At the end of the day, guests leave with little bags or boxes of cookies and little recipe booklets.

Incorporate Italian Wedding Traditions into Your Shower

Introduce guests to Italian wedding traditions at the bridal shower through games and activities, accompanied by explanations and background information. Later at the wedding, while a certain custom is taking place, your shower guests will already know the meaning or origin and will be able to explain it to other guests.

Breaking Glass

Have a big jar filled with broken pieces of glass or glass beads or marbles and have guests guess the correct number of pieces in the jar. The person who guesses the closest wins.

Passing the "Buste"

Provide guests with materials, such as paper, felt, cotton, some scissors, needle and thread, and glue or other adhesive and let each of them make a traditional Italian "buste" or purse. Then, give each guest play Monopoly money to stick out of the purse for fun. The bride can judge which "buste" is the winner.

Tearing the Veil and Cutting the Tie

You can incorporate these two Italian wedding traditions into your bridal shower by providing pieces of tulle and old or cheap ties in the middle of a table or floor. Let your guests see what they can create using these items, and then explain the traditions.

Alternative Italian Weddings

The following wedding themes can also be used for pre-wedding get-togethers—engagement parties, showers, rehearsal dinners, or even for future parties to be held after the wedding.

Venetian Carnival Wedding

A colorful, magical, and festive Carnival wedding will let you and your guests revel in a very specific and well-known Italian tradition with wild costumes, high energy, and many fun activities.

Carnival, also known as Carnevale, is a celebration that takes place in Venice once a year, during the ten days leading up to Lent. The famous pre-Lent festival, with all of its colorful folklore, is an endless parade with festive music and spectacular pageantry. People dressed in elaborate costumes, from the classic white mask, black cloak, and tricorne hat to eccentric ensembles of velvet, silk, with puffy sleeves and enormous hats, fill the Piazza di San Marco. In the evening, merrymakers flock to the town square or pose in the shop windows. They then attend a masked ball, followed by dancing in the piazza.

One of the biggest masked balls is called the Doge's Ball, or Ballo del Doge, and is usually held on a Saturday in the fifteenth-century Palazzo Pisani Moretta on the

Grand Canal. The entire space is elaborately decorated and lit with candles, making for a dramatic scene.

Throughout the week-long Carnival, the streets are alive with parades, street performers, theatrical presentations, and huge crowds. There are musical and cultural events and special art exhibits. Music includes reggae, zydeco, jazz, and chamber music. But the biggest attraction is watching the Carnival revelers in their fantastic costumes.

Among the costumes are historic, Renaissance-looking getups, Fellini-like clowns, the Three Musketeers, and all sorts of disguises. Masks, made of papier-mâché or leather, are worn by almost everyone, and include the popular Portafortuna, the luck bringer, with a long nose and birdlike image, Oriental masks, and various characters of the Commedia dell'Arte. There is also the masculine "Bauta" and the "Neutral," which blends gender features.

The event concludes with fireworks over the lagoon, followed by the tolling of the bells of San Francesco della Vigna at midnight.

You can have a completely-Carnival wedding, or incorporate elements of it into your wedding. Or, hold a Carnival engagement party, shower, rehearsal dinner, or pre-wedding party. Start with guests meeting in a town square or piazza for cocktails and appetizers. From there, move festivities into a ballroom area, such as a large tent, for dinner and dancing.

Have guests come dressed in costumes and masks of their choice, or have them dress normally and provide them with masks. Set the tone in the invitation with images of Carnival revelers. Hire costumed performers to dance to festive music. Host a mask-making party prior to the event or make it part of the beginning.

Ideas for Planning a Venetian Carnival Wedding

Theme and feeling. Drama, magic, spontaneity, "Life is a stage!"

Setting. In a town square, on a blocked-off street, or in another wide-open space (near water is ideal), set up tents and decorate to resemble Venice (see chapter 11) with canals, bridges, gondolas, medieval streets and makeshift town squares, piazzas, and palazzos. Enhance with columns, domes, and velvet, silk, and chiffon scarves dramatically draped. Use both deep and bright hues of blue, yellow, and lavender.

Wardrobe. Elaborate costumes of all kinds, masks.

Music. Reggae, jazz, chamber music, various instruments played by roving musicians.

Favors. Masks, beads.

Activities. Masquerade ball with ballroom dancing, mask-making/decorating stations, face painting, parades, fortunetellers, magicians, costumed performers, musicians, dancers, acrobats, mimes, clowns, jugglers. Event ends with bells tolling and fireworks.

Transportation. Elaborately decorated parade float or gondola.

Romeo and Juliet Wedding

Another theme with an Italian background is Shakespeare's *Romeo and Juliet,* which is set in Verona. The tragic love story was originally written by Luigi da Porto of Vicenza in the 1520s, but William Shakespeare's play is the version that people remember most. It has been made into numerous poems, dramas, ballets, and films, and can be the inspiration for a wedding as well.

Invite guests to your own version of "Casa di Giulietta," Juliet's house, where in the story Romeo climbs the balcony. This set can be re-created with stage props rented from a theater company, or made from scratch.

The setting could be on a stage at a theater or outdoors in a park or garden. You could decorate the rest of the scenery to resemble Verona, the vibrant trading center in the Italy's northeast region of Veneto. The city is known for its rosy pink hue, Roman ruins, and palazzi of Rosso di Verona. The major attractions here are the enormous first-century arena, where many events are held; Piazza Erbe, with its colorful market; and the church of San Zemo Maggione, with its medieval door panels carved with amazing scenes.

Ideas for a Romeo and Juliet Wedding

Invitations. Written on a scroll or a script.

Transportation. Horseback.

Music. Soundtracks from different productions of *Romeo and Juliet.*

Wardrobe. Medieval costumes.

Décor. Make the setting look like a stage. Include balconies, stage curtains, as well as paintings and statues of Romeo and Juliet and Shakespeare. Create a motif of books, quill pens, and parchments scrolls.

Activities. Recite lines from dramatic scenes, hire performers including dramatic actors and ballet dancers to act them out.

Italian Wine-Tasting Wedding

Wine tasting is a popular and enjoyable activity that can successfully be incorporated into a wedding reception. Plus, Italy produces a wide array of great wines, and inspires a winery and vineyard motif that is very appealing for reception décor.

Title your event, "Vinitaly," which is the name of Italy's main wine fair held in Verona in April. You can hold your soirée in an actual winery or vineyard, or you can create the illusion of one at any location, such as a home, courtyard of a museum, gallery, hotel, or banquet room.

The highlight of the event will be a varied selection of Italian wines. How you decide to present the wine is up to you. You can serve a different vintage with each course of a multicourse meal; you can set up wine-tasting stations around the venue during appetizers, followed by a meal served with the main wine; or you can revolve your entire reception around the wine tasting, with stations or bars set up with corresponding appetizers or with a separate appetizer table.

Include samples of sparkling, white, red, and dessert wines, served in that order, as sparkling wines awaken the taste buds and are great to toast the bride and groom with. You can serve the wines of the different regions or you can choose one or two regions (see chapter 9). Select different glasses for each kind of wine. White wines should be served slightly chilled in small, curved glasses, while reds are typically served in large round glasses at a cool room temperature. Glasses in various styles, shapes, and sizes can be rented from party rental stores.

Ideas for a Wine-Tasting Wedding

Suggestions. Serve water with the wine for cleansing the palate between sips, as well as crackers and bread; hire a wine-tasting expert who can teach the guests about the wines they are tasting; provide guests with a list of the wines they tasted.

Setting the mood. Hold the event in the early evening and provide low light with candles, twinkle lights in bushes, plants, and trees; enhance the setting with mirrors; play light jazz music in the background.

Décor. Choose colors such as deep red, maroon, or purple with white or ivory and silver or gold. Use bunches of grapes in centerpieces and decorations and hanging from various places. If possible, use an oak or dark wood bar or bartop. Include art with vineyard scenes and drape flowing scarves around. Include wood barrels, stacked wooden crates, arbors, vines, and ivy. Use wine glasses filled with clear, red, or purple glass marbles and votive candles to accent the room.

Grape designs. Use items designed with images of grapes, which are found abundantly on tablecloths, napkins, towels, dishes, candles and holders, frames, rugs, vases, soap, and other items you might include in your décor.

Favors. Small or regular-sized bottles of wine; wine glasses with bride's and groom's names and wedding date.

Food. In addition to numerous appetizers, your meal might consist only of foods that are made with wine or grapes, or that contain the deep red and purple colors. These may include chicken Marsala, deep red sauces flavored with wine, or pastries enhanced with grape jellies.

Wedding cake. Decorate the cake with a grape motif and bunches of grapes cascading from the top.

Naming wine stations. Name each wine station after the region in Italy where the wines are from or just after random Italian cities. You might also name them after people you know.

Mobster Wedding

Sometimes when people think of Italian extravaganzas, they conjure up images of the glamorous portrayals of the 1920s, '30s and '40s mobsters. You could have a lot of fun planning a wedding based on this theme, and also add an element of early Las Vegas, casinos, big band music, swing, or jazz.

Costumes might include flapper dresses for the '20s, or more conservative knee-length dresses with netted hats for the '30s and '40s. The styles from the '40s feature broad shoulders and cinched waists and glamorous rolled hairdos. And for the men, zoot suits, tuxes, and gangster hats, or leisure suits, silk shirts, and black slacks. Other accessories might include pocket watches, cuff links, pinky rings, gold chains, medallions, long gloves, and long cigarette holders.

You could set up a mock casino, complete with makeshift slot machines and poker tables, and set up a martini bar serving different flavored martinis.

For entertainment, hire showgirls and impersonators of Bugsy Siegel, Al Capone, and the Godfather. As for music, you could play various jazz classics and swing tunes, or you could hire jazz musicians and swing dancers, and even bring in instructors to give guests an opportunity to learn to swing dance.

More Suggestions for a Mobster Wedding

Music. Jazz, blues, big band, show tunes, Duke Ellington, Bessie Smith, George and Ira Gershwin, Cherry Poppin Daddy's, Frank Sinatra, Dean Martin, Harry Connick Jr., Andrews Sisters, Nat King Cole, Ella Fitzgerald.

Transportation. PT Cruiser or vintage Cadillac.

Drinks. Martinis with olives, Manhattans, Cosmopolitans, and Long Island Iced Teas.

Décor. Loungy, dimly lit, chic and glitzy, black-and-white tiles, twinkle lights.

Touches. Balloons, bubbles, disco ball hanging from the ceiling, cigars.

Gifts and favors. Pocket knives, decks of cards, money clips, and diamond toothpicks.

Weddings With Ancient Rome and Renaissance and Medieval Themes

Ideas for an Ancient Roman Wedding

Bridal attire. Straight one-piece tunic to the floor, belt tied around waist. Flame-colored long veil topped with a wreath of flowers gathered by the bride.

Ceremony. Bride and groom join hands and chant "Quando tu Gaius, ego Gaia," "when and where you are Gaius, I then and there am Gaia"; procession includes gaily dressed minstrels who sing and pipe.

Touches. Torchbearers, flute players, trumpeters. Bride-cup is a chalice or vase of silver, decorated with gilt, rosemary, and ribbons. Bride walks with twelve knights and pages. Jewel-studded chalices, robes, canopy, chariot.

Décor. Flowers, bands of wool, tree branches.

Sweetheart table. Backed by a grand colonnade draped with chiffon and twinkle lights and topped with flowers. Surrounded by ficus trees with lights. Large free-standing candelabras, and the table draped with rose and lily garland.

Ideas for a Renaissance or Medieval Wedding

Location. Garden, park, banquet hall.

Décor. Banners, heavy wood furniture, velvet, candles, candelabras, grapevine wreath, white flowers, gold accents, ivy.

Music. Pipe organ, flute, harp.

Wardrobe. Fourteenth and fifteenth century costumes, brocade, lace-up, garnets, pearls, ribbon.

Touches. Parchment scrolls, quill pens, castles, knights, horses, long banquet tables with lettered, colored tablecloths, swords, long-stemmed pewter goblets, drink honey mead.

Transportation. Horse-drawn carriage.

Renaissance décor. Gothic iron arches and quatrefoils; tapestries with garden scenes and tassels; trumpets with colorful banners hanging from them; plaques of knights and ladies; stained-glass windows; decorative shields of armor and weaponry, such as sword and gauntlet displayed on a shield covered in plush red fabric and accented with brass studs; kings' crowns; torch wall sconces; lion statues; gothic angels; dragons; embroidery; tassels hanging from armoires and accessorizing cushions, blankets, and furniture; decorative bows; damask cloth; and golden trim.

Ancient Agrigento Wedding

In the southernmost portion of Italy, on the island and region of Sicily, is a city called Agrigento, which is also known as the Valley of the Temples. This city has its own rich history and culture, which is also very Greek. You could plan an ancient Agrigento wedding, which combines ancient Roman, Mediterranean Italian, and Greek flavors.

Agrigento is filled with temples, statues, and works of art. The landscape is serene and resembles an amphitheater bordered by two hills. The Valley of the Temples features the Church of Saint Nicholas, with a simple and grand facade and gothic and Cistercian architecture.

Ancient weddings in Agrigento went like this: prior to the wedding, an engagement ceremony took place, in which the bride's father promised to give her away to the young man at the wedding. On the wedding day the bride, groom, and a chaperon rode to the temple on a chariot. The bride wore a dress with a long, white peplum with a train and a veil. Guests wore their dressiest clothing, and those who couldn't afford nice clothes would have them bought for them by the bride's parents. The religious and grand wedding ceremony was performed in public.

The bride's family would display all the wedding gifts for the guests to see. During the ceremony, the priest took the bride's right hand and placed it on top of the groom's right hand, and they vowed to live together in happiness. The groom laced a virginity belt, also known as Hercules' knot, around the bride's waist. This was a sign that she was pure and therefore not pregnant prior to marriage. Guests then would throw wheat, barley, and pomegranates at the couple to ensure they would have many children. Choirs would sing and music would play, and everyone celebrated with a huge feast, which was given by the bride's parents in honor of the guests and the gods.

At the end, the newlyweds rode away in a horse-drawn carriage to their new house. There, the cart's axle was burned to prevent it from coming back.

Ideas for an Ancient Agrigento Wedding

Location.   Hold your wedding outdoors, in a Mediterranean-like location, in an arena, stadium, theater, or auditorium.

Attire.   Invite guests to come dressed in Romanesque clothing—togas, long gowns with scarves and shawls, and sandals.

Props. Have guests carry sheaves of wheat. Have floral wreaths available for women to wear in their hair, and have the bridesmaids hold up a floral garland. Other guests could hold up torches.

Décor. Include vases, urns, pottery, stone, draped material, large baskets of flowers, statues, and images of Greek and Roman gods, including Hercules, Juno, and Esclulape. Feature temple-like structures with arches and columns. For colors, go with brights like blues, reds, and yellows. Enhance with golden tones and warm sandstone fixtures.

Other Italianesque Themes

You may also try basing your wedding reception on any of the following themes: Siena Palio, an annual horse race event that takes place in Siena; a Pizzaria Napoli Pizza Party, which is a very informal alternative, serving different varieties of pizza with red and white wine; or an Italiano Extravaganza, which is the total, ultimate, grandiose Italian wedding, with every part of Italy imaginable—almost like your own Italian amusement park. There are limitless ideas for wedding themes and touches based on various Italian regions, cities, festivals, and events. Be creative, have fun, and create the wedding that you love.

Italian Weddings—on Location

AN ELEGANT AND AUTHENTIC Italian wedding can take place anywhere you choose. Planning your wedding close to where you live or where you or your fiancé grew up is a popular and convenient choice, which makes it easy for friends and relatives to attend and allows for a smooth planning process.

However, another option is to take your Italian wedding "on the road." Weddings abroad are a popular alternative, and many services are available to help you coordinate the details.

Certainly, there's no better place to have an Italian wedding than in Italy. Imagine saying "I do" on the hillsides of Tuscany, in an ancient castle in Florence, on a gondola in Venice, or overlooking the Sicilian coastline.

Italian weddings on location are not limited to Italy. There are many destinations within the United States that give the feeling of Italy such as Las Vegas's Venetian Hotel, Bellagio and Caesar's Palace, New York's Little Italy, San Francisco's North Beach District, Northern California's Wine Country, and Chicago's Little Italy. In this chapter, we'll look at the ins and outs of all of these destinations for weddings.

An Italian Wedding in Italy

A wedding in Italy can be the experience of a lifetime. You may have a small intimate ceremony in a town hall or tiny hillside church, followed by a candlelit dinner in a sumptuous Italian restaurant. Or you might plan a full-blown Catholic service in an ornate church, after which you and your guests will celebrate in a palace ballroom with festive music, dancing, and an eight-course catered meal.

A wedding in Italy might consist of a civil, religious, or symbolic ceremony, ranging from traditional to modern, and can take place anywhere, from a church to a castle to a reception hall or villa, in the Italian countryside. It can be a huge family extravaganza or a small intimate gathering.

Several travel agencies offer special wedding packages in other countries. There are also companies that specialize in destination weddings specifically in Italy. Some are located in Italy, while others are in the United States and contract with sources overseas to take care of the many details.

Italian wedding packages can be preset or custom-tailored. Services may include assistance with paperwork, booking wedding sites, accommodations for you and your guests, coordinating the reception, flowers, photography, transportation, hairdresser, makeup artists, and witnesses, providing Jordan almond wedding favors, RSVP service, visits and excursions, wedding dresses (for sale or rental), gondola rides, Florentine guards, horse and carriage rides, gourmet food and wine, videography, music, tuxedo rentals, interpreters, and a wedding coordinator on site for the day of the wedding. Help with organizing the honeymoon is also available.

Sogni Italiani

Sogni Italiani (Italian Dreams) is a company based in the United States that plans destination weddings in Italy according to couples' specific needs. After successfully planning her own wedding in Florence, Chandi J. Wyant created Sogni Italiani to help others realize their Italian wedding dreams.

The company's services range from planning only the ceremony to making all the necessary arrangements. And while Wyant will plan weddings in various cities throughout Italy, she often recommends her favorite city, Florence, and the enchanting region of Tuscany.

Receptions can be as understated as going to a quaint trattoria with a simple but delicious meal and good wine. "This is a great option if you love a lively local feel and a fun atmosphere, with all your guests around one table," Wyant says.

For a more formal ambience, the reception may be held at an elegant ristorante with beautiful décor, frescoed ceilings, and often stunning panoramic views. There the couple and their guests are treated to a gourmet meal with fine wine and champagne as they celebrate around the graciously set table. Even more formal is a reception celebrated in a beautiful Renaissance castle in Florence. The wedding party can secure a private room, with ornate décor and gilt gold chandeliers, and enjoy a catered meal.

For the ultimate wedding reception in Italy, an entire villa can be rented in the Florentine hills (where some scenes from *Room With a View* were filmed). The garden overlooking city of Florence makes an enchanting setting for cocktail hour and/or dinner. Rooms inside are also available.

An important aspect of Sogni Italiani's services is helping clients get through the bureaucracy of getting married in Italy. "If you're trying to slug through it on your own, it can be daunting," Wyant says. "Having gone through it, I can empathize." Using her experience and her ability to speak Italian, Wyant helps clients with the legal requirements of getting married in Italy, including which documents are needed and additional provisions relating to religion.

In some countries, several weeks of residency and/or blood tests are required in order to get married. But this is not the case in Italy.

Many couples also hire Sogni Italiani to plan their honeymoon. Some prefer to spend time in a less touristy spot in Italy and experience the culture, while others opt for more conventional sightseeing. "It depends on the clients' tastes," Wyant says. "I focus on listening to their vision."

Wyant has coordinated destination weddings that have included just the wedding couple or with guests, and she says they tend to be either just the couple or twenty-five to thirty guests, not much in between.

For more information on Sogni Italiani, call Chandi Wyant at (303) 494-4977, email her at chandi@sogniitaliani.com, or visit the Web site at *www.sogniitaliani.com*.

Companies That Specialize in Italian Weddings Abroad

Italy Weddings
email: *info@italyweddings.com*
Web site: *www.italyweddings.com*
Offers civil service or church blessings, provides custom-tailored services, including help with documents, renting villas, and providing catering, transportation, photographers, videographers, hairdressers, flowers, music, wedding coordination, witnesses, interpreter, cake, maps, and directions.

Weddings Abroad/Way Out Weddings
Web site: *www.weddingsabroad.com*
Emphasizes the personal touch; works closely with wedding coordinators overseas. Plans weddings in Florence, Chianti, Tuscany, Rome, Venice, Amalfi Coast, and San Marino. Will add other locations if requested.

Weddings in Italy
email: *info@weddingsitaly.com*
Web site: *www.weddingsitaly.com*
Packages can include Mercedes limousine service, customized bouquets and corsages, wedding dresses for sale or rent,

gondola rides in Venice, music services, photographers, horse and carriage rides, Rolls-Royce transportation, catering, wedding cakes, hairstylists, makeup artists, wedding favors, videography, wedding rings, invitations, announcements, and tuxedo rentals.

Getting Married in Italy by Atlantis
email: *weddings@penteres.it*
Web site: *www.gettingmarriedinitaly.com*
Weddings planned in Florence, Venice, Rome, Siena, Pisa, Tuscan countryside, medieval towns, and the Amalfi coast.

Italia Romantica
Web site: *www.italiaromantica.co.uk*
Helps with paperwork; choosing a location in Italy; books accommodations for couple and guests; provides interpreter, coordinator, flowers, photography, videography, transportation, hairdresser and makeup artist, witnesses, wedding favors, honeymoon, and more. Weddings are planned in Venice, Verona, Tuscany, Umbria, Rome, and the Amalfi Coast.

The Book of Dreams
email: *info@thebookofdreams.net*
Web site: *www.thebookofdreams.net*
Plans weddings in Florence, Venice, Rome, Sorrento, Positano, and more. Takes care of all the details involved in getting married abroad, with services tailored to individual needs.

Rosanna Tours—Weddings in Italy
email *rosannaw@tin.it*
Web site: *www.weddingsinitaly.com*

Check with your travel agent, the yellow pages or the Internet (search words: weddings in Italy) for more sources on planning a wedding in Italy.

Rules for Getting Married Overseas

It is important that you acquire the latest information regarding legal and religious requirements for getting married in Italy, as they may change at different times. While it is possible to complete the necessary procedures yourself through careful research and adherence to guidelines, the process can run much more smoothly with the help of a professional.

Important Things to Know About Getting Married Abroad

❦ Destination weddings are valid and legally binding in the United States, under U.S. statutes. However, each country has its own requirements.

❦ A couple must stay in Italy at least four days before the ceremony.

❦ There are fees, which vary according to the region.

❦ Town hall ceremonies take place Monday through Friday, between 9 AM and 12 PM, and must be booked in advance.

❦ You must have passports or armed forces cards, as well as certified copies of birth certificates. Also, if applicable, you must have proof of divorce or death certificate of former spouse.

❦ Declarations "atto notorio" must be sworn by four people showing they don't object to the marriage under the laws of the couple's home country.

❦ Declaration sworn to by the couple that there are no obstacles to the marriage under U.S. laws.

❦ Passports can take twenty-five business days to arrive in the mail. Check with your local post office, AAA, or other locations that process (and take photos for) passports about forms and documents needed as well as fees.

For more information on legal requirements of getting married in Italy, contact the Italian consulate nearest you, the Italian Government Travel Office at (212) 245-5618, (212) 245-5095, (312) 644-0996, or (310) 820-2977, the local U.S. Embassy or Consulate in Italy, or visit *http://travel.state.gov/italy-marriage.html*.

An Italian Wedding Las Vegas Style

If you can't have your destination wedding in Italy, why not opt for the next best thing? Las Vegas features several sites in which to wed—chapels, hotels, and casinos—and a wide array of things to do. But most important, it features some true-to-life re-creations of Italy.

The Venetian Resort Hotel and Casino

One of the most stunning locations is the Venetian Resort Hotel and Casino, which is distinguished for its Grand Canal and the plaza resembling Piazza San Marco. The Venetian looks like a Disney version of Venice with a canal cutting through the center of the interior, which is crossed by brick and wrought iron-accented bridges.

Guests can ride in elaborate gondolas rowed by costumed gondoliers in black-and white-stripes, straw hats, and red scarves. The canal is lined with cobblestone streets and balconied villas (which are really shops) and topped by a realistic cloud-filled sky.

The Venetian features many replicas of famous Venetian landmarks, including the Doge's Palace, the Rialto Bridge, the Campanile Bell Tower, and St. Mark's Square (pigeons and all). It also offers spectacular meals at five-star and specialty restaurants including Joachim Splichal's Pinot Brasserie, Emeral Lagasse's Delmonico Steakhouse, the Grand Lux Café, Star Canyon by Stephan Pyles, Canonita, Zeffirino, Royal Star, Postrio by Wolfgang Puck, Valentino by Piero Selvaggio, the WB Stage 16, and Lutèce by Eberhard Muller.

Wedding packages include a personal wedding coordinator, and all weddings are performed on the Rialto Bridge over the Grand Canal or on the white and gold Italian gondola. (Contact information: 3355 Las Vegas Blvd., South Las Vegas, NV 89109; phone (877) 857-1861; (702) 414-1100; email *reservations@venetian.com*.)

Bellagio Resort and Casino

The magnificent Bellagio is said to be the most expensive casino ever built. Among its striking characteristics are detailed mosaic floors made of imported Italian tile, glass ceilings welcoming natural light, a glass flower sculpture on the lobby ceiling with 2,000 individually blown glass pieces, and a glass-domed conservatory showcasing fresh flowers and trees. Perhaps most impressive are the dancing fountains in the lake in front, with cascades of water soaring 250 feet into the air.

In addition, Bellagio has a gallery of fine art featuring works by Monet and Degas, an 1,800-seat showroom presenting Cirque du Soleil's *O*, and specialty shops and restaurants including Aqua, Café Bellagio, Le Cirque, Circo, Sam's Olives, Jasmine, Shintaro, Prime, Noodles, Picasso, the Buffet, Café Gelato, Palio, Petrossian Bar, Pool Café, and Sam's Snacks.

The Bellagio wedding chapel is located inside the resort and provides a wide range of services including photography, videography, flowers, spa and salon arrangements, reception information, room reservations, and more. Ceremonies can be performed in German, Italian, Spanish, French, and Japanese. Jewish weddings are offered as well.

Bellagio weddings take place in either the South Chapel, which can accommodate more than 130 guests, or the East Chapel, which seats 30. Both chapels are decorated in soft shades of rose, peach, green, and blue. Wedding packages offer different amenities and all include a video of the ceremony and a box of chocolates. Bellagio is located at 3600 Las Vegas Blvd. S., Las Vegas, NV 89109; phone (888) 987-6667 for hotel information, (702) 693-7111 for attractions, and (888) 987-3344 or (702) 693-7700 for the Wedding Chapel.

Caesar's Palace

Caesar's Palace is the ultimate luxurious Roman experience. This classic hotel and casino opened in 1966, and has remained a lavish kingdom of Roman opulence, with two-story fantasy suites, impressive décor, and an endless assortment of restaurants and shops.

The Palace Chapel at Caesar's Palace features high ceilings with a chandelier, a large stained-glass window, decorative flowers, and room for a piano. The chapel is located inside the hotel, near the Caesar's Palace ballrooms and meeting rooms, which are often used for receptions. Included are various services such as wedding experts, unity candle ceremonies, outdoor ceremonies, reception packages, Jewish ceremonies, guitarists and harpists, flowers, and photography. The Palace Chapel at Caesar's Palace is located at 3570 S. Las Vegas Blvd., Las Vegas, NV 89109; phone (702) 731-7422, (877) 279- 3334.

Vegas Wedding Chapels

In addition to these Italian-themed hotels, several chapels are located throughout Las Vegas, many with an Italianesque ambience. Following are just a few.

The La Dolce Vita "The Sweet Life" Wedding Chapel is located inside the Maxim Hotel, just off the Vegas strip. It features a romantic candlelight renewal ceremony and is renowned for being one of the most beautiful chapels in Las Vegas. La Dolce Vita is located at 160 E. Flamingo Blvd., Las Vegas, NV 89109; phone (888) 625-3869 or (702) 369-9600.

The Viva Las Vegas Wedding Chapel offers traditional and themed weddings of many kinds. Among them is a gangster wedding in a 1940s maffioso style, with "gangster" décor, including red check tablecloths, candles, theatrical lighting and fog, a godfather/minister accompanied by two bodyguards, and a waiter/soloist singing Italian songs. The chapel features a bell tower, vaulted ceiling, stained-glass windows, and room for 100 guests. Traditional ceremonies can take place near a charming fountain or a graceful wrought-iron gazebo. The Viva Las Vegas Wedding Chapel is located at 1205 Las Vegas Blvd. S., Las Vegas, NV 89104. For more information, call (800) 574-4450 or (702) 384-0771, or visit *www.vivalasvegas.com*.

For further information on Las Vegas, contact the Las Vegas Convention Visitors Authority, 3150 Paradise Road, Las Vegas, NV 89109 or visit their Web site at *www.lasvegas24hours.com*. For hotel and motel reservations, call (800) 339-5333; for attractions, activities, tours, and brochures, call (702) 892-7575.

You can reach UNLV Hotel Administration at *www.unlv.edu/tourism/lvmisc.html;* Las Vegas Travel Guide at *www.golasvegas.cc/golasvegas;* Las Vegas Tourism at *www. lasvegastourism.com*.

Italian Weddings in New York's Little Italy

On the lower east side of Manhattan are several narrow streets packed with New York's best Italian restaurants and cafés. This area is called "Little Italy," and is centered around Mulberry Street, from Spring Street to Canal Street, including some of Mott Street.

Little Italy was the setting for the movie *Moonstruck* and its roots are mostly Neapolitan, Calabrese, and Sicilian. Here you will find major sights, including old St. Patrick's Cathedral and the Puck Building as well as Catholic churches, authentic and trendy restaurants, cafés and espresso bars, bakeries, religious stores, specialty stores, gourmet food stores, and quaint shops of all sorts. A traditional San Gennaro festival takes place in September, for which vendors line the streets selling traditional Italian food.

There are several locations within Little Italy to hold a wedding. One of the finest is reputed to be Il Cortile, at 125 Mulberry Street. The restaurant seats 262 patrons plus more in the cocktail lounge, has a private room, and is available for parties and special events. Boasting "good food, good friends, and good wine," Il Cortile features a romantic indoor garden and enclosed skylight for an enchanting setting. For more information, call (212) 226-6060, or visit *www.ilcortile.com*.

Other restaurants (up and down Mulberry, Hester, Broome, Grand, Spring, and Mott streets) include Benito I and II, Buona Notte Ristorante, Caffé Biondo, Caffé Napoli e Trattoria, Caffé Palermo, Caffé Roma, Caffé Sorrento, Canta Napoli, Casa Bella Ristorante, Cha Cha's In Bocca Al Lupo Café, Costa Azzura, Da Gennaro, Da Nico, Due Amici, Ferrara Bakery and Café, Florio's Grill and Cigar Bar, Fratelli Ristorante, Il Cortile, Il Fornaio Ristorante, Il Palazzo, La Bella Ferrara, La Mela Ristorante, Lombardi's, Luna Restaurant, Oniel's, Pellegrino's, Paesano of Mulberry St., Positano Ristorante, Puglia Ristorante, Rocky's Italian Restaurant, S.P.Q.R., Sambuca's Café, Taormina, Umbertos's Clam House, and The Original Vincent's. These seat anywhere from 40–270 guests and feature a wide range of Italian cuisine. For more information on Little Italy, contact the NYC & Company Convention & Visitors Bureau, 810 Seventh Ave., New York, NY 10019, (212) 484-1200, (212) 397-8200 or for the visitor information center (212) 484-1222, or visit *www. nycvisit.com*.

The Manhattan Chamber of Commerce is located at 1555 Third Ave., Room 202, New York, NY 10128, (212) 831-4244, visit *www.manhattancc.org*, or email *info@manhattan.org*. Other sites of interest are *www.go-newyorkcity.com* and *www. allabout-newyorkcity.com*.

Italian Weddings in San Francisco's North Beach

The area dubbed "North Beach" in San Francisco, California, was once known as "Little Italy," and today maintains its Italian flavoring. Here, in a one-square-mile neighborhood, you will find several cafés, old-style Italian restaurants, and shops selling arts, crafts, books, music, gifts, specialty items, clothing, and gourmet food.

One location where you may consider having your ceremony is Saints Peter and Paul Roman Catholic Church. Known as "The Italian Cathedral," this church is located on the north side of the Washington Square, and was founded in 1884. Contact information: 666 Filbert St., San Francisco, CA 94133, (415) 421-0809. Make arrangements for marriages at least six months in advance. Call the weekday secretary for more information.

For your reception, look into Fior D'Italia, located in the heart of North Beach in Washington Square. It is the oldest Italian restaurant in the United States. Fior D'Italia specializes in traditional Northern Italian cuisine and old world hospitality, offers four private banquet rooms for up to 80 guests, and use of the entire restaurant for up to 300 guests. For more information, call (415) 986-1886. And for more information on North Beach and San Francisco, contact the San Francisco Convention and Visitors Bureau, 201 Third St., Suite 900, San Francisco, CA 94103, (415) 283-0177, *www.sfvisitor.org*.

Italian Weddings in California Wine Country

Northern California's Wine Country, which includes Napa and Sonoma Valleys, is an excellent location for an Italian wedding. The scenic vineyards amid rolling hills and sunny skies remind one of Tuscany's Chianti wine region.

Several wedding vendors, coordinators, and specialists throughout Napa and Sonoma Valleys can help you plan the wedding of your dreams at the location of your choice: in one of the area's hundreds of wineries and vineyards; on a scenic bluff overlooking the valley; at a quaint cottage or villa; or in a chapel, church, hotel, banquet room, bed-and-breakfast, or restaurant. Your wedding can be as small or large as you like, and you can incorporate wine tasting into the reception or save it for a honeymoon activity. For wedding sites and specialists, refer to the yellow pages or conduct a Web search via keywords "Napa Weddings" and "Sonoma Weddings." You can also find many photographers, florists, carriage ride and hot air balloon specialists, caterers, hairdressers, and other vendors as needed.

For more information about Napa, contact the Napa Valley Conference & Visitors Bureau, 1310 Napa Town Center, Napa, CA 94559, (707) 226-7459, email *info@napavalley.org* or visit *www.napavalley.com*.

Also contact Napa Valley Tourist Bureau, 6488 Washington St., Yountville, CA 94599-1295, (707) 258-1957.

For more information about Sonoma, contact the Sonoma Valley Visitors Bureau, 453 1st St., E., Sonoma, CA 95476, (707) 996-1090, or visit *www.sonomavalley.com*.

Italian Weddings in Chicago's Little Italy

Chicago has its own version of "Little Italy," featuring several wonderful Italian eateries and shops. Here you can find some great venues for Italian weddings as well. Following are some recommendations.

Maggiano's Little Italy is a warm and welcoming family-style restaurant with Southern Italian cuisine in huge portions with friendly service. There are seven banquet rooms in two locations—three downstairs in the wine cellar and four in the Grand Banquet facility right behind the restaurant—which can accommodate up to 300 guests. The wine cellar rooms are named Belaggio, Barolo, and the Bar Room and have a warm, family-style atmosphere. The Grand Banquet rooms feature an elegant ambience with crystal chandeliers and wall sconces. Maggiano's Little Italy is located at 516 N. Clark St., Chicago, IL 60610. For more information, call (312) 644-4284 or (312) 644-7700, or visit *www.maggianos.com*.

The Como Inn features fine Italian food and a romantic setting. Thirteen private rooms can accommodate anywhere from fifteen to two hundred fifty guests.

Customized services include reception coordination, catering, photography, music, floral arrangements, and more. Como Inn is located at 546 N. Milwaukee Ave., Chicago, IL 60622. For more information, call (312) 421-5222 or email *info@como-inn.com*.

Harry Caray's is an award-winning Italian-American steakhouse that offers casual to fine dining and specializes in steaks, chops, seafood, and classic Italian food. It has three private rooms and accommodates up to 400 guests. It is said to be a great place for a rehearsal dinner. Harry Caray's is located at 33 W. Kinzie, Chicago, IL 60610. For more information, call (312) 828-0966, or email *holycow@harrycarays.com*.

For more information on Chicago's Little Italy, contact the Chicago Convention and Tourism Bureau at (312) 567-8500, *www.chicago.il.org*, or the Chicago Office of Toursim at (312) 744-2400.

You can find many great areas in which to hold an Italian destination wedding. Check with visitors bureaus and tourism centers of locations that interest you.

14

Italian Recipes

As we discussed in chapter 9, Italian food is among the world's finest and most favored, and it is an important part of the wedding celebration and Italian life in general. This chapter is devoted to special recipes for delicious Italian dishes and treats, which can be served at an Italian wedding, holiday celebration, dinner party, or even for a weeknight dinner.

Provided here are a handful of recipes for appetizers, soups, salads, entrées, side dishes, and desserts. Many of the recipes were given to me by my mother, grandparents, aunts, and other relatives and family friends. Some of them I know by heart as I watched my parents cook them through the years, and others grew out of my own culinary experimentation.

Most Italian food recipes are virtually foolproof, granted you pay attention—watching, checking, and tasting and making sure nothing burns. Many rely on a few key ingredients and a cook who can improvise as needed. In fact, some longtime great cooks often measure in pinches, dashes, and handfuls rather than exact calculations. They cook by feeling and have a way of knowing what the recipe needs.

When it comes to popular Italian dishes, most can be made by various methods. While some recipes call for the same basic ingredients, others are subject to as many interpretations as there are people who make them. Many families have their own versions of sauces, pasta dishes, and desserts that were passed down through the years.

Staples most Italian cooks usually have on hand are extra virgin olive oil, garlic, tomatoes, onions, canned tomato sauce and paste, salt, pepper, and herbs like basil, oregano, marjoram, sage, rosemary, mint, and parsley. Also in the pantries of Italian cooks are hot peppers, anchovies, and certainly lots of pasta.

The Traditional Eight-Course Italian Meal

Aperitivo: cocktail
Antipasto/Insalata: appetizer/salad
Minestra, Brodu, or Zuppa: soup
Primo Platto: main course, such as veal cutlets
or roasted chicken
Secundo: a secondary course, such as pasta
or eggplant Parmesan
Formaggi: cheese
Dolce: dessert
Fruitta: fruit, sometimes served with nuts
Caffé: espresso or coffee

Meals are always served with wine and homemade bread.

Appetizers

Note: Antipasto is not part of the everyday meal, but reserved for special occasions like holidays and celebrations. Antipasto means "before the meal," anti (before) pasto (meal).

Antipasto Platter

Marinated mushrooms (about a pound of mushrooms with stems off, soaked several hours in a mixture of 1 cup lemon juice, 1 cup olive oil, ½ cup parsley, and 1 or 2 cloves of garlic, minced).

Mozzarella cubes

Provolone cheese in cubes or sticks

Gorgonzola cheese slices

Rolled thin-cut meats, such as
*   prosciutto or ham, turkey, salami*
*   roast beef, capocollo*

Marinated artichoke hearts

Black olives

Green olives

Pepperoncini peppers

Tomato slices

Pimentos

(Other options include deviled eggs, eggplant, melon balls, anchovies, and pickles.)

Arrange items on platters decoratively and add garnishes of lettuce leaves, basil leaves, parsley, and lemon wedges. Drizzle this mixture—1 cup red wine vinegar, 4 cloves minced garlic, 1-½ teaspoon oregano, and 1-½ teaspoon basil—over mozzarella cubes and vegetables as desired.

Fried Mozzarella

2 pounds mozzarella, cut into thin strips about ½ inch thick

2 cups flour

4 eggs, beaten

2 cups seasoned bread crumbs

4 tablespoons oil (olive or vegetable)

1 cup warm tomato sauce, for dipping

Coat mozzarella strips in flour. Dip coated strips in egg, then coat in breadcrumbs. Heat oil in pan and brown mozzarella on each side. Make sure not to burn, they cook quickly. Serve immediately with tomato sauce.

Fried Calamari

1 pound squid, cleaned well

1–2 cups flour, seasoned with salt and pepper

2 cloves minced garlic

4 tablespoons olive oil

1 cup warm marinara sauce, for dipping

Cut squid into rings or small pieces. Coat squid pieces with flour. Sauteé garlic in pan with olive oil. Add coated squid pieces and fry on all sides until golden brown. Drain on paper towels. Serve immediately with marinara sauce.

Bruchietta

12 baguette slices

1 cup finely chopped Roma tomatoes

½ cup chopped red onion

2 tablespoons olive oil

1 teaspoon basil

Salt and pepper to taste

Preheat oven to 425°. Arrange baguette slices on baking sheet and bake about 10 minutes, or until lightly golden. In a large bowl, mix tomatoes, onion, olive oil, basil, and salt and pepper together and spoon onto baguette slices. Remove baguette slices from oven and spoon mixture over them.

Stuffed Mushrooms

2 cups bread crumbs

1 cup grated Parmesan cheese

2 minced garlic cloves

1 tablespoon olive oil

1 tablespoon parsley

1 teaspoon basil

Salt and pepper to taste

12 large mushrooms, washed
  and stems removed

Preheat oven to 325°. In a large bowl, mix breadcrumbs, cheese, garlic, olive oil, parsley, basil, salt and pepper. Stuff mushroom caps with mixture and place on cookie sheet. Bake until hot and tender, about 10 minutes.

Bread/Pizza

Aunt Leona's Homemade Pizza
the Easy Way

Olive oil
2 loaves Bridgford frozen bread
2 cups onions, minced
2 #2 large cans Italian tomatoes
2 small cans tomato sauce

Salt, pepper, garlic salt, oregano, to taste
1 large ball of mozzarella cheese, grated
Parmesan cheese
Optional: pepperoni, mushrooms, olives

Oil two cookie sheets and spread oil on frozen loaves of bread. Place each loaf on a cookie sheet. Let rise until about 3 times original size, approximately three hours. (Can be left overnight to thaw and rise.) Turn dough over and stretch to size of cookie sheet.

Sautée onions in oil in a pot until soft. Crush and add canned tomatoes and tomato sauce. Add seasonings. Cook over low heat until thick (about two to three hours). Cool sauce to room temperature. Preheat oven to 375°. Spread cooled sauce on dough just before baking. Sprinkle mozzarella cheese, Parmesan cheese, and additional toppings on pizza. (Add pepperoni only during the last 5–10 minutes.) Bake for 20 minutes or until lightly browned on bottom.

Neapolitan "Margherita" Pizza

Pizza dough (either homemade
  or store-bought)
3 cups of canned tomatoes, with liquid
2 cups grated mozzarella cheese
1 tablespoon olive oil

Salt and pepper
1 cup grated Parmesan cheese
2 tablespoons basil
1 tablespoon oregano

Preheat oven to 450°. Roll dough and place on oiled pan. Chop tomatoes and spread on dough. In a medium-sized mixing bowl, combine mozzarella with olive oil and salt and pepper. Sprinkle mixture on pizza. Sprinkle Parmesan cheese, basil, and oregano on top, and drizzle with olive oil. Bake about 15 minutes, or until cheese is melted.

Basic Garlic Bread

½ cup butter, softened
2–3 cloves of garlic, chopped

One dozen dinner rolls cut in half, or a
  loaf of French bread cut into thin slices

Preheat oven to 400°. Mix butter and garlic and spread on bread. Wrap in foil and bake about 20 minutes or until hot. For crispier bread, remove foil and heat in broiler an additional few minutes.

Dad's Garlic Bread
Same as above, but mix butter with ½ cup sour cream, garlic salt, and parsley.

Salad

Note: An Italian tradition was to eat salad after the meal or with the main entrée.

Vinaigrette

2 cups wine vinegar
1 cup olive oil
2 garlic cloves, minced

A pinch each of basil, oregano, salt,
and pepper

Combine ingredients and use as needed.
 Variation: Mix 1 cup lemon juice, 1 cup olive oil, and 2 cloves minced garlic.

Mixed Salad

Mixed greens—iceberg lettuce, romaine
 lettuce, chopped parsley, endive
Tomatoes—sliced Roma tomatoes or
 whole cherry tomatoes

Chopped red onions
Black olives

Options—chopped or sliced cucumbers, carrots, pickled beets, radishes, cauliflower,
red peppers, olives, artichoke hearts, pimentos, capers, grated cheese, croutons.

Soup

Italian Wedding Soup

1 pound ground beef

2 eggs beaten

4 tablespoons bread crumbs

2 tablespoons grated Parmesan cheese

1 teaspoon basil

1 tablespoon parsley

2 tablespoons minced onion

Salt and pepper

Olive oil

6 cups chicken broth

2 cups uncooked orzo or seashell pasta

1 cup sliced cabbage

½ cup chopped carrots

½ cup chopped celery

½ cup sliced spinach

Combine meat, egg, bread crumbs, 2 tablespoons of the Parmesan cheese, basil, parsley, onion, and salt and pepper, and shape into small meatballs. Heat oil in frying pan and brown meatballs on all sides. In a large saucepan, boil broth. Add pasta, cabbage, carrots, celery, and spinach. Return to boil and add meatballs. Reduce heat and simmer about 25 minutes until meatballs are cooked through. Sprinkle with remaining Parmesan cheese.

Pastas and Sauces

Aunt Lee's Manicotti

Dough

6 eggs
2 cups cold water

Pinch of salt
2 cups flour

In a large mixing bowl, beat eggs, water, and salt. Gradually add flour. Knead dough and form fist-sized balls. Roll out into thin round shells, about 8 inches in diameter.

Filling

2 pounds ricotta cheese, beaten fine
A handful of grated mozzarella cheese

Salt and pepper
4 eggs, beaten

Also needed

2 cups tomato sauce
1 cup mozzarella cheese

Parmesan cheese

Preheat oven to 350°. Mix ingredients in a bowl. Spoon filling onto dough and roll into tubes. Arrange in baking dish and top with tomato sauce and sprinkle with cheese. Bake about 45 minutes.

Mom's Stuffed Shells

Sauce

1 ½ cups finely chopped onion

3 cloves garlic, crushed

⅓ cup olive oil

2 29 ounce cans of Italian tomatoes

1 6 ounce can tomato paste

3 tablespoons chopped parsley (fresh)

1 tablespoon salt

1 tablespoon sugar

1 teaspoon dried oregano leaves

1 teaspoon dried basil leaves

¼ teaspoon pepper

1-½ cups water

Sauté onion and garlic in hot oil for 5 minutes. Mix in rest of sauce ingredients. Bring to a boil and reduce heat. Cover and simmer one hour, stirring occasionally.

Shells

1 box large pasta shells

2 pounds ricotta cheese

1 package (8 ounce) mozzarella cheese, diced or shredded

⅓ cup Parmesan or Romano grated cheese

2 eggs

1 teaspoon salt

¼ teaspoon pepper

1 tablespoon chopped parsley

¼ cup Parmesan or Romano grated cheese (for sprinkling)

Cook large pasta shells until just tender. Drain and rinse carefully (trying not to break). Preheat oven to 350°.

In large bowl, combine ricotta, mozzarella, Parmesan or Romano, eggs, salt, pepper, and parsley. Beat with a wooden spoon to blend well. Spoon 1-½ cups sauce onto the bottom of two large baking dishes. Spoon about ¼ cup of filling into each shell, and place shells, topside up, in a single layer on pans. Top with more sauce and sprinkle with Parmesan or Romano. Bake uncovered for ½ hour, or until bubbly.

Fettuccine Alfredo

1 pound fettuccine noodles, cooked
   and drained
2 tablespoons olive oil
2 cloves garlic, minced

1 teaspoon basil
½ cup Parmesan cheese, grated
1 tablespoon butter
Salt and pepper, to taste

In a large skillet, heat oil. Add garlic and basil. Pour over noodles; then add Parmesan, butter, and salt and pepper. Mix well and heat through.

Marinara Sauce

¼ cup olive oil
2 minced or chopped garlic cloves
4 or 5 cups canned or fresh tomatoes
2 tablespoons basil

2 tablespoons basil
Salt and pepper, to taste
1 chopped onion, 1 tablespoon
   oregano (optional)

Heat oil and garlic (and onions, if desired) in large pan. Add tomatoes, basil (and oregano, if desired), and salt and pepper. Stir. Simmer about 30–40 minutes.

Pesto Genovese

4 to 6 garlic cloves, chopped

16 large fresh basil leaves

2 sprigs parsley

6 tablespoons Parmesan cheese, grated

¼ cup chopped pine nuts or walnuts

½ teaspoon salt

½ cup olive oil (do not substitute)

In mortar and pestle or in electric blender, crush or blend all ingredients except the oil to a smooth paste. Slowly blend in oil and stir until smooth. To serve with hot pasta, toss with 1–2 tablespoons butter, adding pesto to taste. Leftovers may be placed in a small jar, covered with olive oil, and refrigerated. Makes about ¾ to 1 cup sauce.

Vegetables

Toni's Mom's Fried Eggplant

1 eggplant, sliced in ¼-inch slices

1 or 2 eggs

Seasoned bread crumbs

Olive oil

2 cloves garlic, thinly sliced

2 large onions, sliced

2 large tomatoes, sliced in ¼ inch slices

12 ounces mozzarella cheese, sliced
   in ¼ inch slices

Pepper

Parmesan or Romano cheese, grated

Dip eggplant slices in egg and then in seasoned bread crumbs. In skillet, heat olive oil and add several garlic slices. Brown eggplant in oil on both sides until lightly brown. Place eggplant slices on a cookie sheet, and top each with slice of onion, tomato, and mozzarella cheese, and sprinkle with pepper and grated Romano or Parmesan cheese. Bake at 350° for 15 to 20 minutes, until cheese is melted and bubbling.

Toni's Eggplant Parmesan

2 eggs

¼ cup milk

3 tablespoons olive oil

1–2 cloves garlic

Eggplant, sliced in ¼–½-inch slices

1 cup bread crumbs seasoned with salt,
    pepper, garlic, and parsley

2 cups tomato sauce

Sliced mozzarella cheese

Sliced onion

Parmesan cheese

Slightly beat eggs and milk in a small bowl. In skillet, heat olive oil and garlic. Dip eggplant into egg mixture, then roll in bread crumbs. Place breaded eggplant pieces in skillet and slowly brown both sides. Preheat oven to 350°. In a baking dish, layer the following ingredients in this order: tomato sauce, eggplant, mozzarella, onion, Parmesan, then more spaghetti sauce. Repeat layers two times, ending with tomato sauce and Parmesan cheese sprinkled on top. Cover and bake for 20 to 30 minutes. Remove cover and bake an additional 10 to 15 minutes, until cheese is bubbling and lightly browned.

LaVonne Marino's (Mimi's) Stuffed Artichokes

4 to 5 artichokes   3 lemon slices
1 cup tomato sauce, thinned

Wash and trim artichokes. Cut off about ½ inch from top of each. Trim tips of leaves. Cut off base. Hit artichoke on top of bread board to open leaves.

Stuffing

Italian bread crumbs   Enough olive oil and tomato sauce
Small amount of minced garlic   to make mixture squishy
    or garlic powder   Black pepper

Mix all ingredients together by hand. Fill center of artichokes with stuffing, then pull leaves back and tuck stuffing inside. Stand artichokes upright in pan. Pour thinned tomato sauce over to almost cover. Add 2–3 lemon slices and cook for about an hour.

Gnocchi (Potato Dumplings)

3 medium potatoes (about 1 pound),   1-¾ cups sifted flour
    cut in quarters   1 cup meat sauce
Pinch of salt   Grated Parmesan or Romano cheese

Cook potatoes in salted boiling water until tender when pierced with a fork. Drain and dry potatoes. Shake pan over low heat for a few minutes. Scald your potato masher or ricer and mash the potatoes. Keep hot. Make a well in the center of flour and add mashed potatoes (should be added when they are very hot). Mix well to make a soft, elastic dough. Turn dough onto a lightly floured surface and knead.

Break off small pieces of dough and use palm of hand to roll pieces to pencil thickness. Cut into pieces about ¾ inches long. Curl each piece by pressing lightly with the index finger and pulling the piece of dough towards you. Gnocchi may also be shaped by rolling each piece lightly off a lowered fork. Bring 3 quarts of water to a boil in a saucepan. Gradually add gnocchi. Boil rapidly, uncovered, about 10 minutes, or until tender. Drain. Add meat sauce and grated cheese.

Meats

Aunt Lee's Meatballs and Sauce

Meatballs

2 pounds ground sirloin	*2 eggs*
1 cup fresh grated Romano cheese	*½ cup parsley*
1 cup bread crumbs	*1 or 2 cloves garlic chopped*
	Olive oil for browning

Mix all ingredients well and shape into balls. Heat the olive oil in a skillet, and brown the meatballs on all sides. Remove meatballs and drain on paper towels.

Sauce

4 large cans tomato sauce

1 eight-ounce can tomato paste

½ pound pork spare ribs

1 pound Italian sausage

Olive oil for browning

4 fresh basil leaves

Add tomato sauce and tomato paste to a big stock pot. Brown pork ribs and sausage in olive oil and add to sauce. Add meatballs and basil. Stir very gently, trying not to break up meatballs. Cook on low heat all day, until oil rises to top.

Stuffed Squid

1 loaf French bread

2 pounds squid tubes

1 large can whole peeled tomatoes

2 large cans tomato sauce

1 can tomato paste

2 or 3 eggs

Parsley

Salt and pepper

Garlic

Break bread up into chunks and dry overnight. Clean squid in cold water and place in a bowl. In the meantime, put canned tomatoes, sauce, and paste in stock pot and heat. While this is heating, mix, with hands, all other ingredients, including bread, in large bowl. Stuff squid with mixture. Be sure not to overstuff as they are plump when cooked. Secure with toothpick (or sew with needle and thread, and remove thread after cooked). Drop stuffed squid into boiling sauce and simmer for 20 to 30 minutes. Handle with care as they burst easily. Drain and serve immediately.

Lori's Chicken Cacciatore

2 tablespoons olive oil

4 boneless, skinless chicken breasts

1 onion, sliced or chopped

4 cloves garlic, minced

1 can chopped tomatoes

1 can tomato sauce

1 cup white wine

1 teaspoon basil

1 teaspoon oregano

1 teaspoon marjoram

Sliced mushrooms and olives (optional)

Heat olive oil in large pan. Brown chicken on each side and remove. In the same pan, heat onions and garlic in oil until tender. Add tomatoes, sauce, wine, basil, oregano, and marjoram (and mushrooms and olives, if used) and stir over medium heat. Return chicken to the pan and simmer about 30 minutes. Serve with pasta.

Desserts

Italian Biscotti

1-³/₄ cup sugar

1 cup margarine or butter, very soft

4 eggs

Rind of 1 orange

1 teaspoon orange extract

2 tablespoons anise extract

3 cups sifted flour (more if needed for firm dough)

3 level teaspoons baking powder

1 cup toasted almonds or walnuts

Cream sugar and margarine and add eggs. Add orange rind, orange extract, and anise extract. Add sifted flour and baking powder, and mix until smooth. Add nuts and spread mixture onto flour board. Add more flour a little at a time to make a firm dough. Preheat oven to 375°. Line cookie sheet with foil and make three long strips from dough. Space strips about four inches apart. Bake for 15 to 20 minutes. Slice pieces diagonally, 1 inch apart, and put back on cookie sheet with cut side up. Cook under broiler a few minutes.

Wanda (also known as Wandi or Fried Bow Knots)

❦

1 tablespoon sugar (more for
   additional sweetness)
2 cups flour
Pinch of salt

3 eggs, beaten
Oil for frying
Powdered sugar, for sprinkling

Mix sugar, flour, and salt in a bowl and add eggs. Mix and knead dough until no longer sticky (you may need to add more flour). Roll into thin pieces and cut into strips. Tie these strips into little knots and lightly fry in pan on both sides. Drain on paper towel and sprinkle with powdered sugar.

Italian Biscuits (Easter Cookies)

8 eggs

8 tablespoons sugar

8 tablespoons oil

1 tablespoon baking powder

⅛ teaspoon anise extract

Pinch of salt

Flour

In large bowl beat eggs until fluffy. Add sugar, oil, baking powder, anise, and salt. Add flour to dough until thick enough to roll, then roll out with hand. Pinch a piece of dough off or cut and shape into cookies (shape as cross, braid shape, bunny shape, etc.).

Tiramisu

5 egg yolks

1-¼ cup sugar

1 cup liquor (cognac, brandy, or orange liquor)

1 cup heavy cream

1 pound mascarpone cheese

9 ounce package or 24–36 ladyfingers

1 cup brewed espresso or strong coffee

1 tablespoon vanilla extract

½ cup cocoa powder

2–3 ounce of semisweet chocolate, shaved

In a double boiler, beat egg yolks in top part of the boiler and add all but two tablespoons sugar. Beat about a minute or until thick and creamy. Boil water in lower boiler and place top part on top. Heat egg mixture slowly, about 10 minutes, while stirring. Beat in liquor.

In a mixing bowl, beat cream with 2 tablespoons sugar (until stiff peaks form). Fold in mascarpone cheese. Pour in with egg and sugar mixture from double boiler.

Arrange a layer of ladyfingers at the bottom of a large bowl or baking dish. Mix espresso or strong coffee with 2 tablespoons sugar and vanilla extract and drizzle over lady fingers. Spoon on ⅓ egg and cheese mixture. Repeat layering ladyfingers, espresso, and egg and cheese mixture. Top with sprinkled cocoa powder and chocolate shavings.

(Note: Mascarpone is a very mild cream cheese available at Italian markets, and gourmet and specialty stores. You can substitute 16 ounces of soft cream cheese mixed with ½ cup heavy cream and ½ cup sour cream.)

Italian Wedding Cake

1 cup buttermilk or heavy cream	¼ teaspoon almond extract
1 teaspoon baking soda	1 teaspoon vanilla extract
1 teaspoon salt	2 cups flour
½ cup shortening	5 egg whites
½ cup butter or margarine	½ cup crushed pineapple
2 cups sugar	½ cup flaked coconut
5 egg yolks	1 cup chopped pecans

Preheat oven to 350°. Grease one large pan or three 8-inch pans. Mix buttermilk (or heavy cream), baking soda and salt and set aside. Mix shortening, butter, and sugar until light and fluffy. Beat in egg yolks to this mixture, one at a time. Stir in vanilla and almond extract. Beat in buttermilk mixture alternately with the flour, mixing slightly. In a separate bowl beat egg whites until they form stiff peaks. Gently fold egg whites into batter. Stir in pineapple, coconuts, and pecans. Pour batter into pan or pans and bake about 35 minutes, or until a toothpick dipped into the middle comes out clean.

Cream Cheese Icing

¼ cup butter

8 ounces cream cheese

4 cups powdered sugar

1 teaspoon vanilla extract

Mix butter and cream cheese together until well blended. Add powdered sugar and vanilla extract and mix until creamy. Spread over well-cooled cake.

Sicilian Cassata

1 pound cake or sponge cake, cut in
    four lengthwise pieces for layering

1 pound ricotta cheese

2 tablespoons heavy cream

2 tablespoons sugar

2 tablespoons orange liqueur

½ cup chopped walnuts, pistachios,
    or almonds

½ cup grated semisweet chocolate

½ cup chopped candied fruit

Mix cheese, cream, sugar, and liqueur in a large bowl. Fold in nuts and fruit. Layer cake with mixture and frost with chocolate frosting, whipped cream, or dust with powdered sugar. Top with candied fruit, nuts, and chocolate.

15

Life After the Italian Wedding

When the wedding ends, married life is just beginning. Following the wedding, there will likely be more wedding-related activities to tend to—the honeymoon, building your new home together, opening gifts and sending thank you notes, viewing your wedding photos and video, and reminiscing about your glorious Italian wedding day.

Afterward, you will be faced with all the wonderful (and sometimes challenging) things married life brings—living together, loving each other, communicating and listening to each other, taking care of the home, planning for the future, possibly raising children, interacting with family and so much more.

The Honeymoon

It has long been a tradition for Italian newlyweds to go on a honeymoon. The couple might leave right after the wedding celebration, usually to a location in Italy or another European country. When they return, they would receive visits from gift-bearing well-wishers for the next several weeks. The gifts, often fine china, crystal, and silver, would remain on an outdoor table to display for weeks.

Nowadays, it is common for couples in Italy to stay home for a week or two before leaving for their honeymoon. During this time, they welcome and entertain visitors and settle into their new homes. Once they are settled in, then they leave on a honeymoon, which can be to just about anywhere in the world.

Planning Your Honeymoon

A honeymoon is a great way for a newly married couple to unwind after the involved process of planning and executing a wedding, to spend some time alone, and prolong the wedding celebration. Even if it's only for a couple of nights, or at a nearby location, the honeymoon is an important part of the wedding activities. Many couples opt to wait a few days after their wedding before leaving on their honeymoon. This allows them time to rest, pack, and prepare for the trip.

Where a couple decides to honeymoon can range from a tropical island, countries overseas, a safari or cruise, to a cabin in the mountains or drive across country. The honeymoon can last for a couple days or over a month. Research the places you and your fiancé may want to go—talk to a travel agent and get pictures and brochures, look up locations in the library, bookstores, or on the Internet, and talk to people who have been to the places that interest you. Find out as much as possible, such as cost, travel details, weather during the time of year you will be traveling, and wardrobe and passport requirements.

For a honeymoon in Italy, or other location with an Italian flair, see chapter 13.

If you plan to travel overseas or anywhere via plane, make arrangements early. It is best to start planning the honeymoon at least four months ahead of time, more if possible. And make sure to acquire a passport at least two to three months before the trip.

Pack smart, take comfortable shoes, and don't forget your camera! Acquire good luggage that is easy to carry/pull, get traveler's checks and/or foreign currency for cash needed for taxis and tips. If you're going to an exotic location or somewhere you have never been, read up on it first, explore as much as possible while you are there, and bring back souvenirs. Most important, relax, and have fun.

Unfinished Wedding Matters

Once you return home from your honeymoon, it's time to begin the rest of your married life together. But first, if you haven't already, you must open all those gifts. Be sure to open them together while keeping a list of who gave you what. You may also have a gift opening party with family and close friends. Either write what the gift is on the back of the card or gift tag, or print out a copy of the invitation guest list (complete with names and addresses) and write the gift description next to the appropriate name. This way, when you go back to write thank yous, the address will be right there.

Start writing your thank you cards right away. You don't have to do them all in one sitting, but do a few now and then whenever you get a chance. You'll be glad you did. On each card, write a personal message, mentioning what the gift is, why you love it, and how you'll use it.

In addition to thank you cards, you may want to include extras, such as wallet-sized wedding photos, a photo of each guest taken at the wedding, or wedding day scrapbooks made from pictures taken with disposable cameras during the reception. Either make an individual scrapbook for each guest, or make one master book and have color copies made.

Official Business

Before settling into wedded bliss, there are a few additional tasks to handle. If you are planning to change your name, you will need to change it on all legal documents—social security card, driver's license, passport, and so on. If you are combining accounts—bank, credit cards, bills, titles on property—be sure to take the necessary steps and fill out the appropriate forms as well. You may also want to order items with both of your names, such as stationery and return address stickers.

Holding on to Wedding Day Memories

Your wedding day is one of the most special days of your life, and there are many ways to make it last forever. You will most likely have had wedding pictures taken to be made into portraits and assembled into a wedding album, and maybe had a video filmed to help you relive this joyous occasion. Other ways to re-capture the day include:

- ❦ Preserving the bridal bouquet. Check with your florist or other specialist who will collect your bouquet after the wedding and preserve it under glass.

- ❦ Preserving your wedding gown. Many dry cleaners offer a service in which they clean the dress and then seal it in an airtight box to keep it from discoloring or becoming damaged.

- ❦ Creating a wedding CD. You, a friend, or the DJ can burn a CD with all of the important songs played at your wedding, such as those played during your first dance, the father/daughter dance, the recessional, as well as Italian songs and others that were played during the event.

- ❦ Creating a memory box or keepsake frame display. You can buy a deep, box-like frame in which to arrange elements from your wedding, such as an invitation, program, picture, wedding favor, cake topper, and your veil, as well as dried or silk flowers if you choose. Display it on a wall as a sentimental and artistic reminder of your wedding day.

- ❦ Compiling a scrapbook. Scrapbooking is a fun and popular hobby these days, with several aisles at gift shops and craft stores as well as entire shops dedicated to it. In addition to (or in place of) the traditional wedding album, create a festive and personalized wedding scrapbook with photos arranged with decorative items, colored paper, and stickers, complete with captions and descriptions. Add your Italian theme to the design of the book with Italian words, sayings, symbols, and illustrations.

♥ Capturing your wedding in writing. Ask a friend who is a talented writer, or hire a reporter from a local paper or a journalism student to observe the details of your wedding and write about it, much like a true wedding story in a wedding magazine. You could provide the writer with the basic information beforehand and emphasize the kind of story you would like. Print the story and frame it or place it in your wedding album or scrapbook.

♥ Displaying your wedding photos. Collect an assortment of your favorite wedding photos—maybe candid shots, those that really capture what your wedding was about or showing different activities—choose five or so, and buy frames that make a statement. They might be rustic and varied, sleek and uniform, colorful, antique, ornate, or modern. Arrange the framed pictures aesthetically on one wall.

♥ Hosting a wedding picture/video viewing party. Invite those who will be most interested in reliving your wedding on film—parents, bridal party, close friends, and relatives. Prepare an Italian meal, or just serve appetizers and cocktails during the viewing and dessert afterwards.

Your Home

Another post-wedding task will be to put all those gifts away. If your home is new and the cupboards are empty, this should be easy. If not, you may need to replace old items with the new, clean out some spaces, and reorganize to make everything fit.

In the old days, an Italian bride would take extra time and care to set up the home with the items from her trousseau—covering beds and tables, filling the kitchen and dining area with china, crystal, and silver, and storing extra blankets and linens in the closets.

When setting up your home together, incorporate important parts of each of your lives—your pasts, interests, tastes, and heritages. You may include family heirlooms, photos, prints and portraits, books, and other favorite items. Create an Italian ambience in your home with furniture, accessories, and artwork. Consider dramatic paint colors on the walls, customized lighting, and unusual light fixtures—ornate lamps and chandeliers. Accentuate your space with live plants and fresh flowers in vases. Consider the following design themes: Mediterranean, Tuscan Vineyard, Romanesque, and Rustic Romantic Old Country. Think ornate, Baroque, or art deco.

Here are some other ways to add Italian touches to your home: inexpensive baskets from swap meets, yard sales, or arts and crafts stores, filled with real or artificial fruits; framed maps of Italy; interesting and unusual wine racks; hanging pot holders; copper pots and pans; hanging dried herbs and flowers; displays of bottles of herb-enhanced olive oil and clear canisters filled with different-shaped dried pasta; grape patterns (fixtures and more); candles and holders; wall sconces; tapestries; wall murals; statues; fountains; stacks of Italian books.

For an Italian Renaissance look, include large-scale furniture, embroidery, gold leafing, stone, parchment lamp shades, stained glass, tapestry, rugs and drapes, and gothic-style chairs.

For a Mediterranean look, feature a mixture of striking shades of blue, green, red, and yellow paired with white.

To capture the look of a Tuscan villa, have a stucco look on the walls, hard flooring such as ceramic tile, stone, brick, concrete or terrazzo, and use colors like moss green, deep golden yellow, soft pale yellow, and burnt sienna.

Create an Italian ambience outdoors with: umbrellas; trellises, arbors, and gazebos with growing vines and grapes; potted trees and plants; romantic porch swings; and Italian flags.

Plant a herb and vegetable garden in the yard or containers on a terrace, patio, balcony, or in a kitchen window, with tomatoes, peppers, onions, artichokes, eggplants, basil, rosemary, thyme, parsley, mint, and marjoram.

Married Life

An Italian woman named Marie once told me, "life after the Italian wedding becomes very normal. There was always visiting the in-laws, which they demanded. The parents are still a very integral part in the married couple's life."

Many Italians say that married life is synonymous with family life. The newly married couple will be expected to gather with family (his or hers or both) once a week, usually on Sunday, and absolutely on holidays. My grandpa considered it close to a mortal sin to even think of not spending holidays with family!

My parents hold a dinner get-together every Sunday for the "regulars," which consists of my immediate family, certain extended family members, and some close family friends. Everyone brings something—wine, dessert, appetizers—and we all sit around the dining room table for a big meal. We always leave feeling stuffed. My late grandfather, Tony, used to sit back in his chair, wipe his hands together, and announce, "I'm bloated!" or complain of symptoms of "agita" (heartburn).

Sometimes the newly married couple's home becomes an additional gathering place—and maybe even "the" gathering place. They can at least expect to be dropped in upon from time to time.

"People do not wait to be invited, Italians just come over," Marie says. "It's just very Italian to stop by a relative's house. It's also very Italian to always have a lot of food on hand, and always have room at the table for an extra person."

Tony G., an Italian who grew up in the Bronx in the '40s and '50s says, "Growing up, life took place around the kitchen table. You would always bring Italian pastry when you would visit someone else's house and they always made coffee for you."

So, if you and your fiancé are from an Italian family, expect to spend many evenings with relatives—at their homes or yours. Make sure to have refreshments on hand for unannounced guests as well. Some visitor-friendly essentials include: freshly brewed coffee or espresso, Italian pastry or cookies (homemade preferred, but from an Italian market will do), fresh bread (with salami and cheeses are a plus), fresh fruit arranged nicely in a basket, pasta, sauce, red wine, and sweet liqueurs.

Tips: know where the nearest Italian market is and invest in an espresso machine, a bread maker, and huge sauce pot (register for these items). Start an Italian cook-book collection.

What Makes a Good Marriage?

For my parents, married thirty-five years, from what I can see a good marriage is undying commitment and being best friends. Long ago, my mom found this saying, which has remained posted in my parents' bedroom over the years: "live like you're in love and you will be."

For Marie and her husband John, married thirty-eight years, it's communication, talking to and listening to each other, being patient. "Nobody's perfect, say kind words and don't be smothering. What has kept us happily married all these years is family and old tradition. We believe in marriage and working at it, and our belief in a traditional foundation keeps it going."

For my grandparents, married for fifty-two years before my grandpa passed away, I suspect it was acceptance, mutual respect, common goals and interests, and tradition.

Tips for marital bliss include: celebrate love and life Italian style every day, cook together, eat together, spend time with family, entertain, gather family recipes, invest in good art, invest in good wine, live it up, express yourself, love and live with passion, learn to play bocci, learn to speak Italian, and attend cultural festivals and events together.

The Holidays

Holidays are very important to Italians, and celebrating holidays with family is a given. Christmas time (Eve and Day) is the most important and festively celebrated holiday feast, followed by Easter and Thanksgiving. Many Italian families have their own traditions and menus they adhere to for Christmas.

One family I know fixes a nine-course meal on Christmas Eve, which includes

Italian Holiday Calendar
and Celebrations

January 1: New Year's Day

January 6: Epiphany

February–March: Carnival

March–April: Lent, Holy Week, Good Friday, Easter

April 25: Liberation Day

May 1: Labor Day

August 15: Assumption, also known as Ferragosto, the official start of the Italian holiday season

September: Feast of San Gennaro (Naples)

October: Feast of St. Francis of Assisi

November 1: All Saints' Day

December: Advent

December 8: Immaculate Conception

December 25: Christmas Day

December 26: Santo Stefano (St. Stephen's Day)

Also don't forget Mother's and Father's Days, birthdays, baptisms, and other important events—all reasons to get together.

baccala (dried fish), salads, and sweets. They also attend midnight mass. On Christmas Day, they dine on lasagna, turkey, and veal cutlet among other things.

In my family, the Christmas Eve tradition has changed a few times over the years. When I was very young, everyone used to gather at the Hall (a rented recreation room at a local park). There would be lots of relatives—from the very old to kids and babies. Uncle Tony (one of many Tonys in the family) would play the accordion, while the kids ran around and the grown-ups talked (very loudly). Tables were filled with all kinds of foods—everybody brought a dish or two. The highlight of the evening for us kids was a visit from Santa—who, unbeknownst to us, was a family friend named Jim—who would hand out personalized gifts to all the kids.

Somehow the Christmas Eves at the Hall faded away, to be replaced by smaller gathering with immediate families. Ours were at my maternal grandparents' house, with my mom's sister and her family. After endless appetizers, including pizza, chips and dips of every kind, hot peppers and olive platters, dinner would consist of sache (stuffed squid), spaghetti, meatballs, roasted peppers, salad, bread, and some kind of additional meat and vegetable dishes, followed by rich desserts and a tray of Italian cookies, anisette, and coffee. Then we exchanged gifts with the grandparents, aunt, uncle, and cousins (Santa and parent gifts would wait until morning).

Now Christmas Eve takes place at my parents' house and includes all the "regulars" for a meal of spaghetti and meatballs or chicken cacciatore, bread, salad, peppers, sometimes stuffed artichokes or fried eggplant, preceded by appetizers of some sort and followed by dessert and coffee. Sometimes squid is served as well, either stuffed or fried.

Christmas Day always did and still does take place at my parents' house. After presents in the morning, an afternoon dinner of turkey, mashed potatoes, and all the Thanksgiving-type trimmings takes place around the table (and additional tables when needed). Of course, dessert and coffee follow.

Easter, which always includes deviled eggs, ham, turkey, and lots of sides, sometimes Easter bread (the twisted kind with colored hardboiled eggs stuck in the grooves), and Thanksgiving with the standard fare also take place at my parents' house—the central gathering place.

Being a Guest at an Italian Wedding

If you are a guest at an Italian wedding or bridal shower, here are some gift ideas for the couple or bride-to-be (mix and match as desired): Italian gift baskets for the Italian cook, consisting of pastas, jars of sauce, spices, cooking pans and utensils, Italian cookbooks, Italian-looking tablecloth and napkins, candles and holders, and so on; a pizza-making basket, with dough recipes, rolling pin, pan, sauce, gift certificates for good pizza place; for the gourmet/wine lover a basket with Italian wines, cheese, sausage, crackers, and other gourmet food items, wine glasses, bottle opener, fake grapes; for the romantic, a basket with Italian chocolates and pastries, sweet liquors, candles, Italian music CDs, bubble bath; Italian picnic baskets and goodies. Other Italian gifts might include a gift certificate for two to a favorite Italian restaurant or a gift certificate to an Italian market; the white satin purse for the bride to use on her wedding day—perhaps with some money inside; Italian leather goods; pasta maker; pizza stone and cutter; lasagna serving dish and spoon and recipe; travel books on Italy; box (or other container) filled with lire for a honeymoon in Italy; wine rack with some bottles of Italian wine; wine-tasting lessons; spice rack filled with spices to use in Italian cooking.

Best wishes for a glorious wedding and a wonderful life together. Remember to always live life the Italian way—to the fullest—and celebrate life together every day. May your love last per cent' anni (for a hundred years)!

Looking Forward

As a newly married couple, you have so many wonderful things to look forward to, such as your firsts together—Christmas, dinner party, home-cooked meal, quarrel and making up afterwards, and many anniversaries. Beyond that, you have several exciting prospects—more anniversaries, holidays, parties, vacations; having and raising children; celebrations and events to attend; helping to plan your children's weddings; grandchildren; wisdom and growing old together and more deeply in love.

On a final note, Italians love to reminisce about their ancestors, heritage, childhood memories, and everyone has a story or a memory about an Italian wedding. Now you will too.

Index